Rut
Management

*Discovering Adventure
in the Routine of Life*

by
Mark A. Cornelius

PublishAmerica
Baltimore

At the specific preference of the author, PublishAmerica allowed this work to remain exactly as the author intended, verbatim, without editorial input.

ISBN: 1-4241-6423-0
PUBLISHED BY PUBLISHAMERICA, LLLP
www.publishamerica.com
Baltimore

Printed in the United States of America

RUT Management
Discovering Adventure in the Routine of Life

by
Mark A. Cornelius

*I hear the word, and see the image...two evenly spaced tracks leading on to some destination determined by someone else's repeated toil. The Phoenicians, the Babylonians, even the Greeks had them. Pioneer America was famous for the Western Trails; romantic notions—symbolic for what we have condemned by a single name— "RUT"—*Mark A Cornelius

About the Title

It's all summed up in a comment by a friend who, when I first told him about the idea of this book commented, "I thought you were supposed to avoid RUTs, not manage them." That's the prevailing misconception, or more accurately, the *misdirection* that inspired the writing. Most of us travel[1] the well-worn path with the expressed mission of "breaking out" of the RUT. And that *seems* to be the right thing to do on the surface, after all; who wants to think of themselves as being in such a routine that they can not, should not, dare not veer off the trail?

---

[1] "live" for you non-metaphorites

But then again, who says regularity and predictable patterns are the training field of monotony and the complacent lifestyle? Does that mean irregularity and spontaneous action are the spawning grounds for innovation and consistent leadership?

I confess to having these corollaries as inappropriately mingled as anyone. I had to stop and evaluate what really influenced me toward the great accomplishments in my life and what type of behavioral patterns truly caused me to crash and burn. I discovered, surprisingly, that the things I hear most promoted—spontaneity, free spiritedness and individual action—are double-edged swords. If left to my own devices, I'm prone to wander from old fad to new fad, never focusing on the distant goal. With the discipline of a constant regimen that strengthens and solidifies me by habit, I become confident in my abilities and at some point, I should be ready to break off toward the "undiscovered" country. The understanding of when to stay in the RUTs (even when tempted to veer off), when to forge new, or when to follow different trails, is what I have coined as RUT Management.

About the Concept

This book offers the RUT as a metaphor to our way of coping with the constant conflict between the "routines" and the "changes" of life. It examines RUT Development, RUT Anatomy, RUT Relationships, and most importantly, addresses the value of RUT Management as a method to recognize the path through RUTs, the way out of RUTs, and the adventure of forging new RUTs. So, this work is not another self-help book designed to cure the RUTted pathology, but instead offers a mirroring tool which recognizes the types of RUTs we may be prone to follow.

At the risk of creating a following, this book will also offer a new RUT Lexicon, some deeper "RUTology," and hopefully, a little RUT humor to make the journey entertaining. It's also meant as a fun but truthful look at the very human tendency to pursue distraction rather than maintain the focused pursuit of long term goals and dreams.

Ultimately, the choice will still be left up to you, whether or not the RUTs you follow are paths still worth pursuing, or if it's time to break out in a new direction. But maybe by examining some historical and personal perspectives—illuminating the fact that there are many more instances where those following RUTs prove to be the true leaders—will give you the necessary confidence to *boldly go where most of us have gone before.* In doing so, I hope you discover as I have, that the best of life is not found in the wilderness, but in the solid and steady progress of the RUTted existence...

...There, I've done it. I've gone and depressed you. DON'T LET IT BE SO! Read on and learn how exciting, not tragic, the pre-traveled path can become. I hope you find this book to be a fresh and fun look at our struggle to simultaneously accept, blend into, and break the molds we recognize as a part of our "RUTine" existence.

And so the charge is given; the challenge presented: In the face of overwhelming monotony, or at the beckoning of the pioneer spirit that whispers to us all, use this information as one more tool in your arsenal to combat the temptation of jumping before the time is right, or hesitating when the real opportunity for course correction presents itself. May the RUT be with you!

Mark A. Cornelius

About the Author[2]

After twelve RUT-filled years of grammar through high school and four years of mundane college life (yeah right), I graduated from the University of North Texas with a double major in Psychology and Vocational Rehabilitation.

---

[2] A friend said that I shouldn't "fake you out" by making you believe I'm someone else writing about myself. So...this will be *me* writing about the author. That's a good thing, because I'm told I'm pretty strange and difficult to understand, so I'm most likely the only one capable of writing about myself anyway.

Upon entering the work world I discovered that my degree choice was probably a subconscious act to help myself, and I was soon well-entrenched in my own vocational rehabilitation.

My journey has included a successful career as an executive recruiter, business development consultant, and wealth management specialist (Don't I sound important and...boring?). My advice is effectively utilized by many in my community except myself, which is why I find the need to write this book and charge money for it. I'm also an accomplished composer and author, whose works are well-known and are now easily overlooked by my community and those closest to me.

I've obviously studied RUTs extensively throughout the course of my education and career, and I've become an expert in their definition, applications, and management—making me the first known RUTologist to be recognized by the esteemed (if unknown) International RUT Association for Management of Big and Loquacious Enterprises (I.R.A.M.B.L.E.).

During this process, I discovered two areas in my life that I can absolutely mess up, but which are correctable to the point that I now consider myself extremely blessed. Those areas are first, my walk with God—accepting Christ as my Savior—and second, my relationship with my very patient family. I give these two sources any credit for my success and apologize for any embarrassment this work may cause them.

Acknowledgments

Editorial Assistance: Thanks to the following for their contributions and their RUT Support. I couldn't have Trekked without you gang!

Vicky Schauer
Chris Slonecker
Stan Tolbert
Tim and Wendy Witherow

Special thanks to my family and friends during my writing time. I know I've been consumed with this project, and yet you've continued to love me. Consider yourselves all loved back.

Finally, thank You God for all that You've done with me. Let this work and my RUT be about Your purpose.

Table of Contents

Chapter One: The Reality of RUTs 11

Chapter Two: RUT Development 17

Chapter Three: RUTology 26

Chapter Four: RUT Relationship 39

Chapter Five: RUT Planning 54

Chapter Six: The RUT Challenge 63

Chapter Seven: A Tale of Two RUTs . . . . 77 and 77

Chapter Eight: Arrival! 87

Index and References 101

CHAPTER ONE

The Reality of RUTs

The secret of your future is hidden
in your daily routine.—**Mike Murdock**

Several years back I was driving down the road to work, thinking of...actually, I don't remember what I was thinking about...and suddenly I realized I had driven a number of miles and had absolutely no recollection of the journey or events that transpired along the way. I'm sure that's never happened to any of you, but for me, a very active thinker and fantasizing-commuter, it was an awakening. The question popped, "Am I just bored? Am I in a RUT?"

"God forbid," I thought. "What a terrible thing to happen." After all, I'm an entrepreneur, a rebel, a...all those "out-front" terms started flooding my gates, and I was afraid I was going to have a wreck while conjuring up the appropriate metaphorical label for my life's work. I pulled off to the side of the road, and as I'm prone to do, I jotted a few notes that might relate to my journal. As I was *curbed*, I noticed the passing traffic and I started thinking dangerous thoughts.

"Am I like *them?*"

"Are they like *me?*"

And I replied with an equally dangerous response,

"Is that a problem?"

Why is being "like" others such a negative concept in our culture? I've read and listened to countless motivational and spiritual mantras about how unique I am and how individually, I can make a difference. I bought it hook, line, and audio CD. But as I watched the day-to-day-ness of the road warriors passing me by, I realized that, although I have unique tendencies, I too, am in the mix of mankind. Though I struggle to be on the cutting edge of things societal—I actually travel a road designed and built by others, to arrive at a destination that they predetermined—long before I ever showed up. And that just happens to be convenient to my very own goals and aspirations.

Yet, we're supposed to shun mass-transit—even despise the idea? Why? Why is being a part of the "throng" a bad thing? Maybe the more complex question is: Are the successful accomplishers, leaders, and managers of the human race exclusively found at the front of the running pack? If the first were true, then the only true leaders of our existence died out long ago, and that would make *all* of us Followers!

Is there another paradigm that suggests a different way of defining the measure our achievements?

▸ **RUT Rule Number One:** *Innovation and leadership are grown, nurtured, and trench-tested in the routine march of mankind.*

In the throes of all my mental gymnastics, I was inspired to start exploring the good, the bad, and the ugly aspects of my RUTful existence. Am I OK with my *sameness*? Is part of my drive to be different unhealthy? Can I actually contribute more to society by flowing *with* traffic, rather than seeking a private path or by trying to drive in the opposite direction? Ultimately, the question boils down to:

Can "Adventuresome Independence" and "Predictable Compliance" live and work

*together as compatible partners in the psyche of
one person?*

The question suggests a conflict and resolution in the same breath. We tend to see individualism and commonality as opposing forces (i.e. two angry momma dogs arguing over a bone for their pups), instead of as two complimentary processes (two momma dogs worn out from arguing over a bone for their pups and now wet-nursing each other's pups), that we all have to struggle to balance as we move through existence.

There is an ongoing debate about the value of maintaining the RUT as a meaningful tool in today's society. From Roman times through the days of the early American pioneers, the RUT evolved from basic fact to nuisance, and from nuisance it wore into a problem, and as such, needed to be conquered rather than respected for its purpose. The "anti-RUTists" may even claim that through the engineering prowess of modern times, RUTs will be totally eliminated, made moot by the individualistic nature of man. The Internet, cell phones, the ongoing decay of the nuclear family, and the emergence of the "Whatever" mentality in our culture each contribute to the idea that "all men are islands" unto themselves. We are encouraged to become more independent and more fiercely pioneering. In such an environment of free-spiritedness and individual rights, a RUT simply cannot, nor needs to function. It should simply vanish into the retirement of an "impractical notion." If you buy that argument, you shouldn't have bought this book (glad you did, I appreciate the RUTful royalties). Allow me to justify your purchase by dispelling this notion.

Paved roads, then as today, allowed for relative comfort, speed, and ease of travel. But soon another problem arose. The un-RUTted road was so nice that the traveler became that much less prone to stray. There seemed to be no purpose in exploration or in risking one's inconvenience upon the natural trail. So, the RUT actually disappeared not at all, and thrives to this very day—simply taking on new form. The truth of which reveals another discovery:

- **RUT Rule Number Two**: *The value of RUT travel must be recognized by the traveler before the journey can become productive.*

After thinking about this a while, I started looking at my own personal RUT for what it is,[3] which led to a simple question:

Is the journey of my RUT properly defined?

The answer required work,[4] and so I began evaluating and documenting the routine of my every day existence. I was astounded by what I found. On a daily basis, I am busy. REALLY BUSY! Even when I'm not busy, there are dozens of things I'm doing or need to do, or thinking of doing, or regretting because I failed to do them or...trust me, I'm busy. And so is everyone I know. Even the lazy people I know are really busy being lazy. A lot of thought and activity are involved in lives, even the lives of those who think theirs are without purpose.

From the simple *beating* of my heart and the *braining* of my brain, to the errands and the obligations and the unforeseen interruptions redirecting me toward new errands and obligations, putting me behind in a schedule that is already behind, causing me to "brain my heart in" and "beat my brains out," it looks chaotic on this piece of paper and not much better...OK worse, in real life. And I was inspired to seek some kind of order to it all. I decided to give it a name. I called it "a Day." You may have

---

[3] Stupid me, I gave a definition to something, so suddenly I'm responsible for seeing if it actually makes sense by applying it to my own life...warning, DO NOT TRY THIS AT HOME UNLESS PROPERLY SUPERVISED AND FORTIFIED WITH CAFFEINE OR SOME OTHER ACCEPTABLE STIMULANT.
[4] Dang!

heard the expression, "Let's call it a Day," or "Man, I've had a Day"—usually punctuated with an exclamation mark[5].

Actually, someone else did that—the "Day" thing. I didn't really come up with the name. I know who did, but that's another story and to stay on track—let's just call it a great idea. The inventor of the Day even went further and defined a series of connected events—Seconds, Minutes, Hours, Days, Weeks, Months, Years, Life—let's call it "Time."[6]

RUT to the Point

We have to summarize the events somehow that have occurred to us, and put them in some perspective and process them to some resolution. But it even goes further than that. At day's-end, week's-end, life's-end, it…the events…all has to make sense to us. Why? I don't know; it doesn't make any sense to me, but it *is* part of the human condition, so I flow with it.

And in "flowing with it," each of us try, in our individual way, to categorize our activities, thoughts, habits, and "stuff." We compartmentalize what we do into some sort of mental "trail" that we can follow to the end of the day and pick up again when we wake up. Otherwise, we'd be even further behind and more disorganized than we already are.

For me, this trail has to be easily found and identified because, in the morning, I usually have difficulty even finding my toes. From the dawn of time, men and women alike have been waking up and, after finding their respective toes, they pick up their trails, and go through the daily routine of life until they are able to pull off the trail for rest, receiving comfort and confidence from the entire experience.

---

[5] !

[6] Also not my original concept

Taken as separate events, the highlights of our individual journeys on the trail vary incredibly (and that's a good thing!), but at the end of the day, when we stand back to observe our accomplishments, it all looks remarkably the same. What do you call the trail? Silly you…

IT'S YOUR RUT!

CHAPTER TWO

RUT Development
(How the "hole" thing got started.)

If you come to a fork in the road, take it.—Yogi Bera

One of the most striking things about RUTs is that they appear to have been designed into the very fabric of humanity. Evidence spans back to the days of Moses, chronicled by the fact that it took him 40 years to get his act together to the point where he was ready to challenge the leading autocracy of the times. Then it took him another 40 years to literally follow the RUT route laid out for him (and the Israelites), to get them to their appointed destination. Along the way, an entire network of laws was laid out creating a very structured social and religious RUT that thrives to this day.

You might ask the significance of historically or archeologically tracking RUTs? Well, RUTology[7] presents the answer:

▶ **RUT Rule number Three:** *Every RUT has an origin and a destination.*

---

[7] Study of the RUT in Motion

The powerful impact of this rule, played out over the course of lives, is illustrated by this example:

Why are railroad tracks 4 feet, 8.5 inches apart?

The English built their railroads to this size, so when America was developing its own railway system, English ex-patriots used the same methods and gauges.

Why did the English build them like that? Their railways were built by people that built the pre-railroad tramways, and that's the gauge they used.

Why did tramways and wagons have that particular wheel spacing? Because wheels would break on the old long distance roads in England if other than the standard wheel spacing was used—because of the RUTs in the road.

Who built the old RUTted roads? The first roads built in Europe were built by Imperial Rome for their Legions. The RUTs in the road were formed by Roman chariots, and everyone else had to match the wheel spacing or else destroy their own wagon wheels. Why did the Romans use this wheel spacing? They used the same wheel spacing because the chariots were just wide enough for two horses.

An interesting twist to underscore my point...the next time you see a Space Shuttle on the launch pad, notice the two big booster rockets attached to the sides of the main fuel tank. These solid rocket boosters are made by Thiokol in Utah. NASA engineers wanted them larger in diameter, but because they are shipped from Utah on the railroad, the boosters must fit through several tunnels.

So, it's interesting that the width of the rails can be traced back to the width of the rumps of two old Roman chariot horses. And today, the world's most advanced transportation system (the

Space Shuttle), is limited by a system designed over two thousand years ago. *Author Unknown*[8]

What's a RUT[9]

OK, I realize at this point that if we aren't picturing RUTs the same way then I might inadvertently lead you down the wrong conceptual path. So before we go too far, I want to make sure everybody's on the same page.

▸ **RUT Rule Number Four: A *RUT defined is a step in the right direction.***

When I talk about being in a RUT, I'm addressing Webster's definition #1:

1. **rut n.** A sunken track or groove made by the passage of vehicles. A fixed, usually boring routine.

I'm not talking about what Webster defines as the following:

2. **rut n.** An annually recurring condition or period of sexual excitement and reproductive activity in male deer.

Surprising as this may seem to some of you, there are others of you who might have been considering definition #2 as the premise for this book. Let me clear the confusion for the "male deer population" (i.e. guys—I'm one, too) who might have been thinking, "What does this book have to do with my sex life?" I assure you not a whole lot, unless your sex life is in a RUT. If that's the case, you'll have to absorb the rest of this book with illustration in mind. I will not cater to your imaginations.

---

[8] Which possibly means I invented this premise, but wanted to give it third-party validity. Actually I didn't invent this—found it on the internet quoted anonymously possibly meaning someone else invented this premise and wanted to give it third party validity.
[9] Or if you prefer, "RUT's a What?"

On the other hand, I pose a question based on a connection between both these definitions. Who of you have heard the term, "I'm in a RUT"? Most of us (I believe) attribute this phrase to definition #1, signifying that the routine and boring stuff is bad and to be avoided. Actually (grammatically and historically), the term "To be in a RUT" is coined from definition #2, implying a hormonal circumstance on which I won't elaborate.

It does, however, suggest one of those quirks of language where one statement is improperly associated with another event and thereby the definition or implication is altered. To defend RUTology properly, I now venture into new territory and suggest another redefinition. I say, keep the phrase

"To be in a RUT" associated with definition #1, but conceptualize (well, maybe not, how about visualize...no, co-mingle...definitely not; let's try AFFILIATE...YES!), affiliate the meaning with the excitement we attach to definition #2. I can only hope this technique is beneficial and acceptable for both genders.

I offer this wordplay because it helps illustrate the problem. As a culture, we have made the RUT a bad thing, when culturally it is one of the most prominent and potentially productive aspects of our existence.

▸ **RUT Rule Number Five:** *RUTs are a part of life, get over it!*

Before delving too deep into the realm of the RUT, I thought it might help for me to give an example of a real-life RUT, one that clearly portrays the mundane, repetitious, and mediocre progression that most of you associate with the term. And so, I present for your reading pleasure—let's see, whose life would be average enough, yet compelling enough to capture the hearts of the book buying public, oh yeah—My RUT!

(Please find some sad violin solo to play in the background. It'll help create the mood.) To save time, it was in my teens that I discovered a love for music and for creative writing. Amazing for someone diagnosed with lysdexic...pardon me...dyslexic tendencies in grade school. Nonetheless, when I had a pen in my hand and ultimately a key board, I discovered happiness. I *thought* from that point forward that my ultimate goal was to become either a famous song writer who would pen the greatest novel ever written. So I trudged innocently into my future, thinking naively, that all I would have to do was to write a few great pieces, show them to a few great people, and PRESTO...I'd be a famous writer.

Reality was somewhat counter to my ambitions. First, there was college. I first thought that I wanted to be a music major. That was a huge mistake. The college path of music at that time had only two destinations in mind: Music teacher or Super Classical performer. I was neither, nor was that my desire.

I switched to Psychology and found a home. I understood this—I connected—I could do it and prosper! The only problem was that it didn't seem to fit into my ultimate goal of writing, which even during the busy college years, I strived to develop. I even wrote a musical that was taken on tour, shown in a prominent music theater in Houston, Texas, and ultimately produced as a record album. Still, such efforts did not pay the bills so I entered the world of work.

I won't bore you with my career path except to say that I ultimately gravitated to sales consulting. I'm happy and successful in my work, but it's not my driving passion—you now know my passion! Along the way, I've written many songs, several more musicals, plays and the like. I've created a journal blog that has gained popularity and, of course, within these pages unfolds my latest endeavor.

But something was missing. I felt like I had been in a "RUT"—as defined earlier...the negative kind—and that I wasn't getting closer to my goal. Yes, I had a RUT for sure, but no clearly defined plans, no discipline (I confess I tend to be lazy, wanting desperately for others to do my work for me) and most importantly, I had a *misinterpreted destination*. I had thought that my goal was to become "successfully famous," when actually, as I discovered far later down the path, I really wanted to become "famously successful." In other words, I found out that my joy was in doing the very best work I could possibly do in my craft. My desire for fame was in the "doing-of," not in the "recognition-from" my writing.

That changed things dramatically because now, I could choose any vocation with which to feed my family and prove myself reliable. Don't get me wrong, vocation and income were—and still are—extremely important components of my RUT because without them, I couldn't support my family or…my habit. Not only that, everything I had pursued—the psychology degree, the consulting career, my family, and even the music—was all part of a connecting trail that led me to this point. They all influenced and contributed to my purpose and as I looked back over that entire part of my life, I could actually see how my RUT had gotten me here. Viewing that progression in hindsight became an even greater inspiration to trust my RUT to lead me to where I wanted to go in the future, even though there might be confusing or discouraging points along the way. Suddenly, my RUT looked like a brand new vehicle that could take me exactly where I wanted to go.

The challenge now became how to balance my vocation with my family time and my thrilling outlet. I had to manage the routine of each area, and to do that, I needed a solid plan that would grow with me and help me reach my real destination…which I've discovered is:

To share my experiences through the written word, in a high quality, entertaining fashion, with whomever will read and appreciate the words that connect us.

Looky there, now I was "RUTting!" But as I looked even more closely at my new RUT, I realized that it actually was my old RUT. It hadn't changed…I HAD! My attitude, my approach, my respect for my RUT had all redefined themselves into something positive and exciting, and THAT was the "new thing."

THAT is something to write about and share with others!

A Fresh Look

So how do I redefine my RUT to help me look at the road ahead with a positive focus? For that purpose I RUT back[10] on an age-old remedy: the Acronym.

The RUT is not just an image, but a process by which we think and base our actions. It is also, by its very nature, a verb that defines the noun; so I'm in a RUT and I'm RUTting concurrently. My observations of the RUT uncovered not only movement and purpose, but intent toward a destination. Therefore, in my attempt at nomenclature, I've had to "cheese-ball" all of these ingredients into a single description. And the result is...

Repetitive **U**nchanging **T**rajectory syndrome[11]

---

[10] Yes, RUTs do travel two directions and so can their occupants. Stay tuned for a related RUT Rule later in the book!

[11] I hesitate to use the "s" word in capitalized form because, sure enough when I do, some "psych-type" will claim RUTOLOGY as a legitimate science and will soon find that both themselves and their patient load are in a whole new RUT called "Sessionology," causing hourly rates for their newfound RUT specialization to be increased and then I'll have to write a whole new book about Trickle Down RUTonomics, spinning me into a new RUT called "Sequelology"...and we just can't have that, can we?

The misperception of the RUT is in its repeating pattern and its foreseeable outcome. The problem lays in my very human ideas as to how a RUT works. I think of a RUT as a repetitively cyclical pattern.

I HATE repetition because I think it "locks me in"…

…Trapping…

…and the fact that I know where the cycle of the RUT is leading me…

…Tracking…

…sends me right over the edge, with my only desire being to reverse or take off in a new RUT direction, trying to re-RUT the very plan I originally accepted as "mine"…

…Trailing…

…even though I claim that I'd like to predict and then "RUT Manage" my own future…

…Trending.

The traditional perception of the RUT cycle can also be illustrated in graphic form:

How predictable, how…regular and ordinary! And what a paradox! I desire a certain outcome to my planning, but once the course is set toward that objective, I sense an imprisonment of my own creation and so I rebel against my own desire. That's why my goals can so quickly become redirected from my original desire, to that of simply escaping my RUT. In other words; my perception of being entrapped changes my mindset to one of "escape," rather than viewing my circumstances as preparation for some destiny I seek "down the road a piece."[12]

RUT to the Point

As a matter of fact, the bottom line of this entire chapter centers on the fact that there is no syndrome attached to a RUT, meaning you shouldn't go and make yourself (Or let anyone else make you) sick over a false concept. So, as you and I begin to redefine our perceptions of our RUT, it's critical to remember…

‣ **RUT Rule Number Six:** *RUTs are not to be considered diseases or dysfunctions, but rather as central to the way we "get on" with life.*

You've had a peek now at someone else's RUT and although every RUT does share common characteristics, *my RUT is not your RUT*. Now it's time to redefine and find the value of your own RUT so that you can manage it properly. It's by the recognition of the RUT as an exciting and fruitful place to exist, that we begin the journey toward self-fulfillment in its most productive form. So go ahead, ***get over it and get on with it!***

---

[12] Fancified Texas colloquialism for "in the future."

CHAPTER THREE

RUTology
(The Good, The Bad, and the RUTty)

Not everything that is faced can be changed,
but nothing can be changed until it is faced.
—James Baldwin

A pastor of a church I know quoted an anonymous writer[13] as saying, "A RUT is just a grave with both ends open." Obviously, this guy hasn't studied RUTology as *in-depth* (sic) as I have. Otherwise he would understand and appreciate the difference between a RUT and a PIT. Indeed, it's a grave mistake (sicker) to automatically assume anyone's entrenchment as a static situation.

About now you are asking, "What in the world is this twerp talking about? I have no idea what the terms he's throwing out mean in the context he's using them." Not to worry. I'm about to remedy all of that by defining the true essence of the RUT and its occupants.

In Chapter One, I started by defining my idea of a RUT. But what if the very idea of being in a routine or of following, rather than leading, offends someone's personal values? The difficulty is in finding "Po-RUT-ically Correct" terminology that resonates with everyone. Our pastor friend is a great example. He not only

---

[13] Which possibly means he invented the quote but wanted to give it third-party validity?

formed an opinion based on someone else's quote and mindset, but his view then became part of his entire belief system, so that when he now hears the word "grave," he thinks, "RUT." And when he thinks "RUT," he thinks "dead" and…on and on. What a PIT[14] he now finds himself in. And with this guy's influence, he has now telegraphed his interpretation to a whole flock of eager ears who thinks this boy hung the moon. So now they believe what he believes, and are tragically trapped in the same PIT! Whatever are we to do to help?

What if…someone, say a fairly competent if unknown writer, were to replace the offending words with imagery and a social concept that speaks to the truth and balance of "routine"…make that "RUTine" and "exploration"? What if, in doing so, a new perception is created that redefines the personal and societal RUT-Walk, causing people to recognize the value of a disciplined (if seemingly unremarkable) life march? Would they latch onto and embrace the idea as a revelation into their personal, moment-by-moment lifestyle? Would their (and my) perception of a RUT suddenly be turned upside down and cause *real* personal change? There's only one way to find out…

▸ **RUT Rule Number Seven:** *The only way to remedy a negative cultural (or individual) image is to redefine it, causing a re-imaging of popular thinking.*

To help the personal RUT-Walk make sense to all, we have to all be able to make sense of and follow the road signs and map keys. Otherwise, some of us would end up in Topeka,[15] when we wanted to be in Nashville. Therefore, it's vital to know and agree on the right terminology.

---

[14] Don't worry, this acronym too shall be defined…be patient.

[15] No offense meant to you Topekonians. It's a beautiful town, and there will be a book signing in your area soon.

As a matter of fact, the word "Walk" doesn't really work in the RUT World. A better description would be "Trek."[16] We're about to explore a number of new terms that will help keep your "RUT-speak" straight. And to help you not to have to flip back to this chapter later on to search for a definition, I've included (ingeniously) a RUT Lexicon at the end of the book for your reference pleasure. Now that the stage is set, let's do some RUT lane changing!

In Chapter Two, an endlessly cyclical pattern of the RUT was portrayed by association with the very human reactions of: **Trapping, Tracking, Trailing,** and **Trending.** Now, with a stroke of the pen, this all too familiar pattern is redefined to present a more positive "stair-step" approach to the RUT. Instead of a repeating cycle, I now view the Trek as a series of accomplished RUT Steps toward an ultimate destination. Here begins Mark's view of...

RUT Reality

Instead of perceiving the word *"Trapping"* as one that locks me in, I now consider the RUT as a confidence-building and skill-developing guide that produces a sense of...

...Reliance

From this frame of mind, understanding the *track* on which I'm being led makes me less anxious, more excited, and even looking forward to a well-managed and meaningful outcome...

...Relevance

---

[16] Say it with me, "RUT Trek." Very good, let's Trek on.

I now become less escape-minded in my approach because I know why I'm heading where I'm heading. And instead of *trailing* back over previously trod ground,[17] I start again to consider my original objective...

...Realization

Now, in place of wanting to predict my own outcome, I can readily embrace the idea that I am preparing as best I can—in the immediate moment—for what I can't possibly see *trending* beyond the horizon...

...Revelation

The Progression of RUT Steps in graphic form:

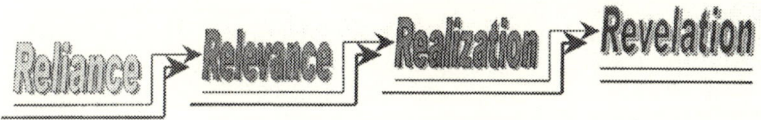

OK, I know. Just coming up with snappy ideograms and charts is only a start, and by themselves mean nothing, unless there's an active culture or society that acts out the meaning. So, here comes the big one:

---

[17] Or becoming sidetracked by wanting to escape rather than moving forward with a purpose.

RUT Image

How I walk...oops...Trek, is not by following what actually "is,"[18] but by interpreting what I see based on some sort of belief system—good or bad. The closer the screen of my cerebral cinema is to reality, the less likely I am to bump into the walls of my RUT[19]. The less bumping, the less I have to engage in Rest Stops to clean up. The less Rest Stopping, the less risk of them turning into PIT Stops,[20] thus, the more efficient and effective becomes my RUT Trek[21].

▸ **RUT Rule Number Eight:** *I get a whole lot more accomplished—a whole lot faster—following, rather than fighting, my RUT.*

And that's the key. Think about a time when you've had a work project to complete or some chore requiring a little more creative effort than that of the normal Neanderthal "kill and eat" strategy. For example, let's say the project is cleaning up and reorganizing your office, or a room in your house, and that the task must be completed within a nine-hour deadline. If you're anything like me (God help you), the operation goes something like this...

8:00—8:15 AM—Daydream about the final outcome of the project and of the accolades you'll receive from friends,

---

[18] Refer to Clinton, William Jefferson for the proper definition of "is."

[19] Rut-Bumping implies my careless attempts to randomly escape my trek with no intended purpose.

[20] No, I STILL haven't stated the meaning of a PIT...on purpose...to annoy you!

[21] Avoiding RUT Bumping also saves a great deal on dry cleaning bills which greatly improves the RUTonomics of my life.

family, your boss, and the Nobel Peace Prize Committee for a job well-done.

8:15-8:45 AM—Start sketching out your ideas for how you plan to accomplish your clean-up goals.

8:45—9:15 AM—Read your plans as you sit and stare at the piles of "stuff" that you need to go through, only to realize you have less time than you need, which means you start thinking about all of the other activities you'll not have time to do if you stick to your plan.

9:15—10:30 AM—Begin the clean-up process, all the time regretting your commitment because you now perceive that your true objective was to come up with the plan and then coerce someone else into doing your work for you[22].

10:30—11:15 AM—Consider the options available for a lunch break, because you know that if you get away from the task-at-hand for a while, you'll be better able to design your organizational strategy.

11:15 AM—12 Noon—Hurriedly box-up all objects that "look" like things you probably won't use and carry them out to the trash before you change your mind.

Noon—1:30 PM—Over lunch, discuss with a friend/co-worker how much you've accomplished. Now that you feel so good about your progress, you allow yourself to be talked into staying an extra half-hour to discuss...anything but the project. Your friend/co-worker explains that they have just bought a new car that is better equipped than yours. You immediately request a test drive.

1:30—5:00 PM—The ride goes famously and you decide your real goal for the day was to buy a new car. You

---

[22] See The Adventures of Huckleberry Finn by Mark Twain if the idea of coercion appeals to you. If you don't have time to read this incredible classic because you're busy reading my book, buy Huck Finn as a gift for someone else and have them tell you all about it.

drive to the dealership and spend the next three hours in the price/negotiation/need/justification and capital sacrifice phases of your vehicular love affair.

5:00—7:00 PM—Drive…anywhere, until it's too late to do anything more about the organizational phase of your project, which you think was a stupid idea in the first place, because you now have this new car and that's going to require you to work harder to make the payments. So you really don't need to reorganize any longer because you're going to be too busy going places in your new car, which helps you justify the purchase.

Yes, it's an allegory, and yes, it's a stretch to take a day's activities and use them as a life lesson, but when I honestly take the time to look at any long-term effort I've started which has been temporarily or permanently shelved, in most cases, I find that the same pattern emerges:

> *It's not because of outside or intervening circumstances…*
> *…It's not due to a lack of available resources…*
> *…It's not for a lack of planning or initial commitment that I'm distracted, or completely derailed from my track;*
> *It's because…of ME!*

I know why I purposely sabotage my own directives. After all, I was the one who cooked up the ideas in the first place. Nevertheless, I often fail to **Rely** on the plan with which I started my Trek. Why? Because I didn't believe in its **Relevance** toward my long term purpose. What's the proof of my doubt? My ability to be easily distracted and side-tracked. I seldom pause to remember that…

…my purpose has power.[23]

If I had faith in my objectives, I would recalibrate the way I approach them in order to keep the RUTine manageable, and at the same time, challenging and exciting. How? How can I **Realize** the "sameness"…and allow it to become an enticing pathway to be pursued passionately over the long run? Simply put, I need to periodically look beyond my current task to imagine its completion and the positive consequences of its success!

▸ **RUT Rule Number Nine:** *RUTs need management because they are much less intentional than they appear.*

Now that I've *got* how my RUT *gets* "screwed up" down pat, let's explore why my image of a plan—my RUT Path—gets so mixed up. Could it be nothing more than a choice? Is my RUT the preferred route to my dream spot, or a poorly planned tour bus ride to someone else's paradise? Do I have a say in the pursuit, or are there limits to my control of the path? Well, of course there are limits, it's a path—it has boundaries, and if I choose to follow the path, I've got to accept its limitations just as readily as its opportunities. On the other hand, there are a number of things I *can* choose and control about my RUT. It's pretty simple really, I can choose to:

* Stay in the RUT—**RUTting**
* Turn back and retrace my RUT route—**Back RUTting**
* Stop temporarily to rest and get my bearings—**a REST Stop**
* Become fixed in a specific location, undecided about the best direction to continue—**a PIT Stop**

---

[23] Once I turn on the engine of my new car, it becomes more than just my new toy to admire; it's a vehicle to take me places!

- Veer off my RUT onto another established RUT route—**ReRUTting**
- Veer off my RUT into completely unexplored territory—**Trail Blazing**

These definitions appear self-explanatory, but each can have a huge impact on the success of your Trek. Each option you choose is critical to your final destination.

RUTting: We've already defined and explored the stigma attached to this phenomenon. I say, let's show the skeptics what a "RUTty" bunch we are!

Back RUTting: Usually indicates fear or doubt, but sometimes can be the trail of someone who wants to re-examine their path in an effort to determine if their future course is right for them to continue to follow. Chapter Five will look into ways to use Back RUTting as an effective tool when necessary.

REST Stop: Yup, just like it sounds. Sometimes, especially on a long Trek, you've just got to stop to get your bearings, coffee-up, and…we don't need to dwell here…you get the picture.[24]

▸ **RUT Rule Number Ten:** *Rest Stops are not Pit Stops.*[25]

PIT Stops: Now that we've broken the ground of consideration that maybe RUTs aren't all bad, and very possibly the best track for a successful journey, it's time to look at the dangers of the well-traveled road.

---

[24] Aren't you relieved I didn't elaborate?

[25] Yes, finally your patience has paid off, oh tenacious ones. See next section for the definition you've been waiting for.

Repeated travel on the RUTted road leads to a very well known phenomena...PITs:

Periodic
Interruption of
Trajectory...

...those nuisance makers, those portions of the trail so worn by use that the Trekker becomes slowed, even stuck in position. PITs are not RUTs, but are a dangerous by-product of a well-traveled RUT, especially where lots of **Back RUTing** has been involved. A PIT is to a RUT Trekker, like an open manhole is to the traveler on the road. Hit it just right...and suddenly you are a permanent monument in the traffic of life.[26]

As a matter of fact, PITs are often confused with RUTS, which for the most part, explains why RUTs have gotten such a bum rap in the first place.[27] Safe to say, a PIT Stop is best avoided, no matter the temptation.

▸ **RUT Rule Number Eleven:** *The existence of a RUT proves motion, which is a good thing. PITs imply immobility and stagnation, which are very bad things.*

ReRUTting: Nothing wrong with setting a new course under the right circumstances. We'll examine those in Chapter Five as well. The problem is with those of us who hop from one RUT to another with annoying regularity. You know who you are out there. I infrequently peruse your infomercials claiming the latest,

---

[26] Want a good example of a PIT? Do you know anyone so consumed with television that they schedule everything else in their life around their favorite programs? Ouch, that may hit a little too close to home!

[27] The even greater danger is that a PIT, just like a RUT, can become totally habitual—thus becoming a *Permanent* Interruption of Trajectory

greatest remedy, gadget, or system ever invented until the very next latest and greatest...blah, blah, blah...replaces yours next week. Yes, there are people who actually make a living out of changing directions for the purpose of coercing others to also change their direction. The trick for me is to constantly remind myself that MY RUT TREK SHOULD NOT FOLLOW THAT OF PROFESSIONAL RE-RUTTERS.

Trail Blazing: Ah, this is where we all THINK we want to be headed—off the beaten path, out into the great unknown, free-ranging,[28] pioneering—these terms are typically used to describe the entrepreneurially inclined attributes of those reading along—myself included. The problem is, WE'RE WRONG! Even the pioneers were sage enough to realize that the best way to get to the new world was to follow the tracks of someone who'd already found and marked the undesirable elements along the trail.

There are countless stories about countless[29] enterprising individuals such as J. Paul Getty, John D. Rockefeller, Thomas Edison, and others, who started out with nothing and built empires on pure genius, going where no person had. But did they go where no one had gone before? Nope. They used the trial and errors of others (as well as their own) to methodically carve out the juicy little corners of their fabulously wealthy individual universes.

▸ **RUT Rule Number Twelve:** *A RUT Trek takes its direction from the direction someone else established ahead of you.*

---

[28] Terminology particularly dear to health-conscious chickens

[29] The word "countless" bothers me. Why define something that can't be done? Why did I even use the word? Forget it.

And there's the rub, Shakespeare. As much as we'd all like to think of our singular efforts as exclusive, there is more evidence to the contrary. But LOSE NOT HOPE!

> **The real discovery is not the creation of my uniquely individual RUT, but in the RUT I choose to follow that starts me on the path toward becoming a unique individual.**

How can I stay committed to Trekking *my* RUT, when I'm not even sure it's the right RUT at the right time? Ah yes, the challenge that eventually faces every RUT Trekker at some point along the journey. Even if I accept that I am in a RUT, my attitude associated with my Trek may come under **RUT Conflict,** because society tells me that the attitude I take toward my RUT depends heavily on whether or not I'm at the beginning of the RUT path, smack-dab[30] in the middle, or at a strategic RUT jump-off point. I argue that my attitude should stay consistent, because my objectives should never change no matter where I'm positioned on the Trek.

RUT to the Point

So many allegories, so little time to Trek…

As the value of RUTs are further outlined and the actual techniques of RUT Management are laid out, we'll unearth more terminology that will help make the journey easier to traverse. Meanwhile, it's important not to get too wrapped up in the fear of traveling a *Bad* RUT vs. negotiating a *Good* RUT.

---

[30] Tennessee colloquialism for a Texas colloquialism—"Up to my boots"

It's in the "internal (mental) image" of the RUT
that I either choose to celebrate or curse my
existence.

That's why having the proper language to better define, and run with the overall image of your Trek, is critical. RUT Dissonance[31] will no longer be a part of the positive RUTology embraced by the enterprising readers of this book, nor will your attitude toward your RUT be pessimistic. Because now, with your definitions properly aligned: *Relying* on a new way of *Realizing* your direction's *Relevance*, you are well-prepared to RUT with a passion as yet unimagined,[32] and are ever nearer to your *Revelation* of what the *change in attitude* toward successful RUT Management is all about!

---

[31] RUT Dissonance—The argument that goes on in your head that suggests you might have made a mistake in your choice concerning some aspect of your RUT, also fondly known as "blowing your brains out from the inside."

[32] Those of you still stuck on definition #2, keep your images to yourselves.

CHAPTER FOUR

RUT Relationship
(RUT Characteristics
and the Characters who share them)

No RUT in the mind is so deep as the one that says
"I am the world, the world belongs to me,
all people are characters in my play."
—Donald Miller

It's taken me years to recognize and admit to the power, and very real influence, other people have on my life. The most telling evidence that I am not alone in the world looms before me in the very tracks of my RUT! The trail already laid out ahead of me is a constant reminder of a greater truth:

If your parents don't have children, neither will you.

Why do I perceive cohabitation of the planet as a problem? Shouldn't I be glad for the company? What is the RUTology that compels me to yearn for an independent, rather than a codependent, path to success? The answer lies in the ultimate

RUT destination—my Epitaph. I don't think I'm much different from most people in what I want inscribed on my tombstone:[33]

> "Incredible guy, this one: He made a unique contribution to the world, going where no man has gone before and staying there for long periods of time, until others caught on, realized he was a brilliant pioneer, and so they followed."

I wish I could say that I am totally in control of the things around me, the events that shape me and the outcomes of the things I'm involved in...but, it would be self-deception to say so.

▸ **RUT Rule Number Thirteen:** *RUTs by definition are designed for more than one person to Trek.*

Before jumping into the tracks of any RUT, there looms a nagging question: How do I even know "this is the RUT to be Trekked" in the first place? After all, there are so many from which to choose.[34] If I stand back for just a minute to observe my past habits and disciplines, I find that I first saw someone else doing what I've done, or I followed a system that was in place

---

[33] Ladies, please don't be offended by the following inscription. My intention isn't to ignore your contribution to this illustration. Here's how I'd like you to join in. Wherever in this book you see the words "guy" or "man," please replace with "girl" or "woman," "he," substitute with "she," etc. It'll be really fun, a very interactive exercise; you'll see. Men, I invite you to invert in the same manner where I might have used a feminine example. That should pretty much fix the world we cohabit. On the other hand, if you're inclined toward breaking out of your respective RUTs; keep the language the same; embrace the opposite personal identifiers as the "new you." That should liven things up a bit.

[34] To the ladies out there; it's like picking a shoe store to visit at the mall. Men... A mall is a big building full of lots of stores that are all the same and...never mind, it confuses me too.

that worked nicely, adopting it as my own. Maybe I even got clever (it happens) and I added some new procedure, or I found a unique way to do the same thing in what looked to be an innovative way. And, coincidentally that's how I determine my future RUT. The only way I'll know if the RUT is right, is to peer up ahead for people in need of followers, companions, or sometimes even leadership—waiting for me to catch up to them in the RUT they've already created—and then start aiming toward where they have already Trekked! Another simple bit of RUT Wisdom:

Someone was here before me; otherwise there would be no RUT to follow.

Now is about the time I could get really dramatic about the bitter reality of my commonality, throw up my hands, and scream out loud, "What's the use, there's nothing new under the sun!" And again I'd be wrong.[35]

In 1881, a dedicated group of people approached the United States government with a request. This group was led by a very quiet, but remarkable woman who was not known as a leader, but more of a servant. She had decided seven years prior, after doggedly pursuing a rather unremarkable career RUT as a copier in the U.S. Patent Office, that hers should become a life of volunteerism. She proceeded to seek out ways to help others in an already existing cause, and in doing so, identified a great need that was being debated and addressed internationally. Instead of re-inventing what already existed, this maven gathered together

---

[35] And besides, all the rest of the people at the mall would turn and look at me, then call security on me and I'd have to make up some lame excuse like, "I couldn't find a popular brand of bath soap in the Body Works Shop" because it's been bought up by all the other men who are in their RUTs trying to please their wives who are in their own RUTs trying to smell nice for their RUTting husbands (Definition Number One you perverts).

like-minded individuals and presented the idea of simply following an example already being implemented in Europe. They created nothing novel, invented nothing new, but in their zeal to help mankind, Clara Barton and her supporters formed the American Red Cross. It was based on the same model already exhibited by the International Red Cross, but because of her tireless efforts and ability to patiently observe, learn, and mirror the actions of her mentors, her suggestions and innovative approach to the idea of serving humanity's healthcare needs, both in war and peacetime, quickly thrust Clara into the forefront as a leader of this great movement. Not only did the US government grant her request, she then became the inspiration of the entire world to re-examine and develop protocols for the largest and most successful health organization the world has ever known.[36]

Because a RUT path is already well established doesn't mean that another, following the same route, can't display originality—digging in to discover fresh RUTovation by smoothing out the twists and turns along the way to make the Trek easier for those who follow—which brings up another revelation about the nature of the RUT...

Even though the path and direction are set, the landscape of a RUT changes because of the travelers who touch it.

And not only do the travelers change the RUT, but the RUT also changes the traveler. One significant and dynamic example of this is the morphing of followers to leaders, and leaders back to followers all along the Trek. Maybe, just maybe,[37] I'm moving at a different pace and with more or less energy in my RUT than

---

[36] Perspective based on the following source material: www.informatics.org/redcross/history

[37] OK, maybe it's more than "maybe", maybe it's "definitely," because I just hit you with a great historical example of my upcoming point!

those who have preceded me. I might even pass others up who are in the same RUT as I am. Why at times, I might even jump into the very lead of the RUT I inhabit!

▸ **RUT Rule Number Fourteen:** *A bunch of us can be at different locations in the same RUT at the same time.*

How do followers become leaders? How do leaders move into the role of followers? How exactly, can I establish my individual identity, while taking the opportunity to learn from others on the same Trek within the confines of my well-worn route?

RUT Unity

Popular culture is full of statements about team building and cooperation, but it's seldom portrayed in such a way as to build up the other guy's agenda first. As a matter of fact, team building oftentimes discourages any self-interest—mine or theirs. OK, fine, let's win one for…for who…the organization, the company, the team? Who in the world *is* the team?[38]

The "team" is a bunch of individuals secretly wanting to achieve their own personal objective using the resources of the team, which is geared toward a common objective that typically does not have a thing to do with the individual's desired secret objective.

Cynical? Maybe, but look at the way teams are formed. They are put together for the purpose of solving a group problem, which most likely was identified by one or two people who may not even be associated with the team (other than at its inception

---

[38] Oh, oh, here comes "Counter Culture Mark" doing his "thang."

and membership appointment). Thus, the team originator's objective becomes the driving force behind the team's purpose—and even its very survival.

Inevitably, individuals on the team will have some other need they think can be woven into the fabric of the prime objective. The problem arises because it is assumed (by the very essence of team formation) that the prime objective is…the prime objective.[39] But because individuals inside the team are…individuals,[40] they will frequently place a greater value on their secret need than they do on the prime objective, thereby slowing down, re-routing, or even derailing the team's original purpose.

Will you find this hypothesis in any team building books? Never! Why? Who would want to admit such a thing? How could anyone accurately measure such a thing? How do I know this happens? Easy… ***tell me I'm wrong!***

Now, before you e-mail me to death with your responses, ask yourself this question:

> ***If I could help someone else with their need, sacrificing my own need, would I?***

And, like me, there will be a bunch of you (to your credit) who will not hesitate to say, "Oh yes, of course"…as long as…

> ***… "there is a real need"***
> ***… "there is time"***
> ***… "there is value"***

Wait a minute. Wouldn't those three conditions imply that I'm making the rules? What about the team? There should be no "self-service" in this equation. But there is…

---

[39] Duh
[40] Duh #2

And before you start blasting me with "Nasty-Grams" about my insensitivity and your impression that I have no idea what I'm talking about, consider the following:

> *If I could first help someone else with their need, and in doing so also meet my own needs, would I?*

Where are the connecting conditions to this question? Isn't the very nature of helping others also in some way helping myself…even if the need served is to feel like I've served the need? Is that not still injecting my interests into the mix?[41]

Fine—Now that I've really got your agitators spinning—let's go for the heart of the RUT relationship issue:

> *RUT Servitude—the concept of cooperatively helping others achieve their goals and destinations while simultaneously reaching out for our own brass ring.*

"Back up," someone out there is saying. "Isn't the concept of 'serving' all about putting other people first?"

That's right, what's so confusing? Servitude is sharing whatever one has with another for the primary benefit of the other. It's the very reason why RUT Trekkers don't hide their tracks. They WANT to serve; they WANT to be on a team; they WANT to travel as a pack. THAT'S THE WHOLE IDEA!

▸ **RUT Rule Number Fifteen:** *Teams are not about teams; they are about others.*

Near the beginning of this chapter, I asked how leader and follower roles could become juxtaposed. I also said I'd explain

---

[41] Burn, brain cells, burn. I can smell the smoke from here!

how an individual could remain unique within the confines of the RUT walls: Ready for the answer?

RUT Synergy: I have to be willing to let others in my RUT pass by me in both directions, realizing that there may be another, more capable of leading than I am, who may be **RUTing** up from behind. I may have to let a former leader, who is no longer able to lead, **Back-RUT**. I can't be willing to do this so that I can move faster through the RUT, but so that the RUT works more effectively for all involved. RUT Synergy results in RUT Unity. It's really what teams were meant to be, only better...RUTtier!

RUT Influences

Since we're talking about the congregational aspects of the RUT, let's tackle this one—it's to RUT Followers I now speak: Another reality of RUTs is that for every leader on the edge, there are many who are meant to (and need to) be passengers on the wagon train. If we are all truly out there forging new trails, there would be (make that "are") way too many paths to choose from. Someone has to follow.

To the stalwarts who must find ways to make the "New Way" work and who then continue to refine the New Way until it becomes the "Old Way," and suddenly find themselves Trekking the common ground known lovingly as their RUT...to you I say (and this is the tough one to swallow)...

...FOLLOWING IS OK.

There are many times when I'm smacked with the awareness of *someone's* or *something's* repetitive influence over my life whose influence has led me down a road I didn't even know I was traveling. I would be less than honest if I didn't say that these moments of revelation make me uncomfortable and that I typically resent the surprise of not realizing I have arrived at a destination prior to the understanding that I've been steered toward that point. Yet, can I claim these manipulations to be always harmful or damaging? Maybe to my ego, but if I'm blatantly forthcoming and again fall back on history for my measure, there have been at least as many (come on Mark, be honest...) OK, there have been MANY MORE times than not, when these discrete RUT influences have bettered me, rather than set me back.

Ask any well-founded person about the times their father or mother[42] resorted to the patient and methodical trickery of "parenting" in order to impart a life-long lesson. Did the individual even know there was a classroom involved? The key to my success in negotiating a roadmap that someone else has helped to construct, is in the management I apply as I navigate my RUT. In other words, I make sure that I'm looking at the entire picture, so that I can gain the proper perspective about where I am and where I'm going. This is where Rest Stops come in handy—pausing just long enough to seek out the positive influences of other Trekkers—while at the same time keeping a watchful analytical eye out so that I'm not sucked into some *cross purpose* imposed on me by another Trekker who may not have my best interest at heart[43].

▸ **RUT Rule Number Sixteen***: The original creator of a pathway had their own purpose or destination in mind.*

---

[42] Remember, without these individuals, this example would be mute...VERY mute...as in nonexistent.

[43] Another Texas phrase that seems to capture this notion is also, amazingly, found in Mr. Webster's handbook. The term I refer to is *bum steer*—Part of Speech: *noun* Definition: incorrect information. Synonyms: bad advice, bad information, bad tip, poor advice, poor guidance, poor information, poor tip. Sentence use: Eating that six-day-old unrefrigerated hamburger was a bum steer.

The important question is... Where is the RUT taking me?

RUT Conflicts

So what about those frightening examples where the subtle encouragement of lock-step thinking or regurgitated rhetoric, results in whole societies of robotic pathology? Wasn't Nazi Germany a great example of a major RUT gone bad?

Of course, any sociological tendency can be abused, mutating its impact into something unintended.

Yet, there are the shining examples on the other side where the well-RUTted society has won the day. Ancient Greece, Ghandi's India, and the United States stand out as shining socio-political examples of how a mass of people can Trek together knowing that by RUT Servitude, they truly can help themselves by first helping others. Said another way...

You really can lead by following.

Are there RUT Trekkers who want nothing more than to follow, who never strive for any forward position on the journey? Sure, but they don't define the "majority" in the RUT race as some would have us believe.

▶ **RUT Rule Number Seventeen:** *Good or bad, RUTs are so defined by their travelers, not by their direction.*

Indeed, the RUT is designed to direct and strengthen each traveler along the path. If individual Trekkers choose only to follow other Trekkers just for the sake of following, with no other purpose in mind, they run the risk of becoming snarled in traffic as all the other Trekkers pass them by. Soon they become either trapped in place, or stopped out of frustration or fear due to the rush of passersbys—and suddenly they find themselves in the confines of a well-established PIT!

If you run across these folks on your Trek, by all means take a Rest Stop and encourage them to move on with you. But, do NOT hang around too long! As happens many times in RUT travel, the sojourners stranded on the side of the road may look innocent enough, but sadly, they aren't interested in moving on at all. They really just want permanent company to share in their tragedies. If they aren't willing to Trek with you, MOVE ON QUICKLY, or risk becoming a member of a potentially lifelong PIT tailgate party.

Speaking of ulterior motives along the RUT path, what happens when leaders or followers who want to take on the mantle of leadership decide they see a better direction—a direction that no one has taken before? What happens when "the" RUT, or any RUT, just won't do?

The contradiction of RUT Trekkers vs. Trail Blazers

Earlier, I presented the idea that one can become a leader while still entrenched in an existing RUT. Does this mean that pioneering and rugged individuality only exist in the form of front, middle, or back positions on an existing trail? NO WAY!

Far be it from me to reject the idea that exploration is such a one-dimensional process. Ironically, this book exists to suggest a broadening of perspectives, encouraging not only the Management of RUT Trekking, but also honing the discipline necessary for the rugged individual to break ranks altogether.

I've been privileged to meet, observe, and work with a number of unique souls who do not wait for anyone to tell them how to proceed or succeed. These men and women appear (and indeed may well be) unafraid of circumstance and consequence, thus leaving them seemingly impervious to the outcomes their actions generate. Ask such people if they are happy and they'll describe events or times when everything was nearly perfect. But their ongoing level of self-dissatisfaction and their desire for higher accomplishment is ever pushing them to "find another way," a "new and different way." And this is the standard held up by mankind (and by most business success publications) that we are all to strive to become. Call them the *Trail Blazers*.

There have been plenty of articles spewed forth about the wonders and romance of Trail Blazing, but the Trail Blazer[44] is truly the minority on the planet, and a fairly dysfunctional bunch of socializers at that.

Dysfunctional yes, but critical to the cause of RUTology because...

▸ **RUT Rule Number Eighteen:** *Without Trail Blazing there is no RUTting.*

It's the natural course of things. First, someone has to explore the unexplored. Then, someone else has to confirm that the unexplored has now been explored. Then, other people need to catch up to the first explorer and see what all the fuss is about. Finally, they tell their friends all about it and voila—A RUT IS BORN.

This concept is nothing new—we just need someone or something to follow. What is perhaps a remarkable consideration is the idea that...

Every Trail Blazer has also been a RUT Trekker.

---

[44] Sorry, this is way off track, but every time I say the word "Trail Blazer" I get this image in my head of those old 1950-style Westerns with the cowboys dressed in filigree and rhinestone jackets—i.e. the Trail Blazer. Just throwing that out in case there are others of you with warped minds who are also wandering off about now, daydreaming about similarly twisted associations.

What? You're not impressed by the depth of this comment? "Give me something more profound," you say? OK.

Every Trail Blazer was first a RUT Trekker.[45]

They would have had to have been a RUT Trekker just by the definition of their role. After all...

▸ **RUT Rule Number Nineteen:** *To break out of a RUT, you have to be in a RUT.*

Current world culture has indoctrinated me with the idea that each of us has a Trail Blazer within, and that my desire to tame the unknown territory is the end all and be all. I need...we all need to be the one out in front...the Marine on the beach...the Scout in the wilderness...the Prophet before his/her time...Elvis before...no, I refuse to go there.

The bitter pill...we, the majority of us—*me, myself,* and *I* included—are not built to be true Trail Blazers. Leaders yes, thrill seekers maybe, but there are differences hardwired into the fabric of the true "Free Spirit" that make them...unusual unto themselves.

Trail Blazers by their very nature need several things to thrive:

1. A clear, unblemished landscape on which to roam unencumbered
2. A cause/destination not easily reached by normal activity, that when achieved/reached is perceived to benefit themselves and/or others
3. Followers to clear out and make sense of the rough swath left behind by these Plow Heads

---

[45] There would obviously have to be ONE exception to this rule—i.e. the Inventor of the RUT whom we shall acknowledge in a later chapter.

They aren't meant to be many in number. It's a lonely job made more so by the hardship and frustration encountered along the way. And, even though Trail Blazers were at one time "of the crowd," once they break away, it's extremely difficult for them to re-acclimate to become again, travelers of an established RUT. Like the carnivore who's tasted fresh meat,[46] nothing else will do, and so the very existence of the Blazer becomes synonymous with finding the next undiscovered territory, rather than fulfilling a long-term life purpose.

Most of us are just simply not up to the task of Trail Blazing and that's a very, very good thing because of the huge cost attached to such a lifestyle. Most of the individuals I just described are on second, third, and fourth marriages, many lacking true friendships, and all complaining of a sense of constant impatience for the next BIG event in their lives.

▸ **RUT Rule Number Twenty:** *RUTs are forged by others to be followed.*

In other words, Blazers don't and can't do well in a crowd. And the rest of us, though we thi.nk we'd like to be alone,[47] don't function well for any extended period in isolation. The paradox of RUT Trekkers and Trail Blazers is that we *need* each other, but we can seldom *be* each other.

RUT to the Point

Whether we examine RUT profiles on a mass scale, or under the microscope of intimate one-on-one relationships, RUTs only work when shared. What allows some people to be blindly and

---

[46] Not to be confused with "bum steer."

[47] Especially during the early morning ear-splitting days of crying baby parenting.

habitually coerced toward disastrously deviant behavior, while others unify and march boldly and willingly into the construction of great establishments? The key is in the recognition of RUT *benefit* and RUT *detriment*.

In the identification of how my RUT works, helps, or hinders me, I become better able to recognize the times to follow along, accepting my entrenchment, or when it's time to break away from the pack and discover a new path. The identification of my RUT's qualities, and the directional choices I then make based on that information, are the "Main Streets" of RUT MANAGEMENT.

CHAPTER FIVE

RUT Planning
Making the RUT Management Connection

The solutions all are simple—
after you have arrived at them. But they're simple
only when you know already what they are
—Robert M Pirsig

Oh boy, now we're getting somewhere. I've been spouting off for four chapters on what RUTs are and are not. Now we get to talk about my favorite subject, the very one this book is titled after—RUT MANAGEMENT[48]. This is the part where I connect the dots. For example, in Chapter Three we spent a lot of time on RUTology, especially about creating an image that allows us to see RUT Trekking for its positive application. If you buy into this concept that you possess the skill of RUT Imaging, which is the ability of mentally looking forward and backward to honestly define the track of your journey and effect its outcome, then you're ready to read on.

▶ **RUT Rule Number Twenty-one:** *I choose my RUT, my RUT does not choose me.*

---

[48] Or, "How do I do that Voodoo I do so well?"

The first step in looking at how to manage my RUT is to decide first which RUT is mine. To help figure this out I took a trip back in time to the year 1958, the year of establishment of the National Aeronautics and Space Administration...

...This unique organization is forged out of unique circumstances. Sputnik is already in orbit, and the United States is heavily engaged in what they believe to be a race for dominance in outer space. Four military branches, a separate group of scientists, and the United States Government are all vying for the option to lead (and therefore control) this new frontier. New technologies are being invented and tested at breakneck speed and no one has a complete picture of the best approach to the problem. For that matter, the problem—other than "being behind the Russians"—isn't even defined!

Behind in what—what have the Russians done other than place a tin can in orbit? What is the goal? Is our goal their goal? What does outer space have to offer in terms of opportunity and who is best suited to tackle the initiatives? Combine this with an alarming rate of failed launch attempts of experimental rocketry, personnel injuries, and deaths, and it becomes very clear that structure has to be wrestled from chaos.

NASA's methodical "Think Tank" approach to safe and efficient space exploration became a universal model for problem solving, and launched a dynamic development program unparalleled in the history of scientific study.

Their commitment to a systematic approach of space exploration still exists today, because of the time spent early on in determining exactly what path the administration was to follow. This is reflected in NASA's first mission statement:

To advance and communicate scientific knowledge and understanding of the Earth, the solar system, and the universe and use the environment of space for research. To explore, use, and enable the development of space for human enterprise. To research, develop, verify, and transfer advanced aeronautics, space, and related technologies.

The path was rugged, the territory virgin. Success followed failure and failure followed success.

But because of their determined approach in an environment that invited great risk, right along with great revelation, names such as Apollo 1 & 13, Challenger, and Columbia were (and are now) honored as unfortunate, but necessary sacrificial stepping stones that helped augment, not deter, the successes of the Mercury, Gemini, Apollo, Space Shuttle, Space Station, and future exploration projects.[49]

Preparation

NASA...now THAT'S the way a RUT should be built! They did what is so difficult for any of us to do when faced with multiple life choices, career paths, desires, and interests. They stood back and took the time to ask:

Where do I want to go?
Where do I want to end up?
What am I willing to do to get there?

But wait, there's more, they took it one step further. This is what I had the greatest difficulty doing before I discovered RUTology. Instead of plowing ahead once they had determined their ultimate goals, NASA then asked (and forced themselves to answer) the toughest question of all:

---

[49] References from NASA website at www.nasa.gov and from www.eadshome.com/NASAmission.htm.
Commentary by Mark A Cornelius

> *What am I willing to sacrifice and to not do in order to keep focused on the RUT I've chosen?*

Answering these questions is one thing, but then comes the twist in the road:

> *Just because I can recognize my RUT and even decide about complying with, or rebelling against its course for my destiny, doesn't mean I'll manage my Trek well.*

I must have the discipline to keep plodding along the path of preference. Back to our Bubble Headed NASA friends for point of reference: Had they the benefit of this book in 1958,[50] they would have first considered the question in Chapter One: *Is the journey of my RUT properly defined?*

In their case, NASA laid out their direction using a traditional Mission Statement. This method is still real popular these days and works as long as people can easily recite and therefore "internalize" their belief statements. In NASA's case, I suspect not many of those early folks, if asked by someone passing by, "Hey NASA person, what's your purpose?" would immediately have spouted off, "Well thank you for asking! I'm here to advance and communicate scientific knowledge and understanding of the Earth, the solar system, and the universe and use the environment of space for research...blah, blah, blah."

------

[50] I mean, think of it. The fact that I could have even written this book at the age of four would have been totally amazing and I would have become incredibly famous and rich for doing so, but besides that, imagine if NASA had had the benefit of this approach already written instead of having to figure it out with slide rulers and all those mechanical pencils stuck in their lab coat pockets. They would have been light years ahead of their already stupendous progress!

Then again, being geeks, maybe they did, which is why only the astronauts got the girls. Doesn't matter, it seemed to work for the geeks and maybe they didn't want the girls. Personally, I prefer the "Image" approach I outlined in Chapter Three, because it's something I can see in my mind. Even if the words I use to describe my RUT change, my passion and conviction never do, and THAT'S WHY I CAN GET OTHER PEOPLE EXCITED ABOUT JUMPING INTO MY RUT![51]

Now, this is where it gets tricky. There were some people that NASA would simply not want to have RUTting along with them. How do I know this? There are people I don't want RUTting with me, and I know people who don't want me RUTting with them. That's good…REALLY!

For example: I personally would be uncomfortable RUT Trekking with a bunch of Olive Brine Testers.[52] With great respect poured out to the dauntless followers of this career path, I simply would not have the stomach to endure the tales they must constantly share relating to the PIT stops frequently encountered. Each of us has similar "undesirable associations" that we try to avoid included within our Trek, and there are similar disincentives which keep us from changing to other RUTs. Chapter Four spoke about relationships and their importance to RUTs, but…

▶ **RUT Rule Number Twenty-two:** *To be successful, the right people at the right time all need to be properly RUTting for any given RUT Trek to be successful.*

To put it another way, just because people can Trek my RUT doesn't mean that people should Trek my RUT…and visa versa. The wrong people together in the wrong place at the same time

---

[51] Actually, I had trouble getting girls too, but at least I WANTED to!

[52] Dictionary of Occupational Titles code 522.584-010. Reference www.occupationalinfo.org/52/522584010.html

can confuse or completely obliterate a perfectly good RUT. One tool I've learned to use to help me decide if I want to invite someone to Trek Along is a short True/False instrument I call THE TREK TESTER[53]. It involves a few quick statements I throw at the people that I believe I want to associate with, to see if they're also prepared for the Trek:

MARK'S TREK TESTER

- **True or False: *You are in a RUT.*** (Their answer should be *True*, otherwise they are, or they want me to think they are a Trail Blazer...don't need any of those on my Trek. If they answer *False*, skip the rest of the questions)

- **True or False*: "You" can change the direction of the RUT that "I" follow.*** (Answer; *False*. If I invite those who answer *True* on my Trek, I'd experience lots of RUT Bumping before their ultimate ReRUTting because they had another pathway in mind when they jumped in with me. Why did they enter my RUT at all? Probably they were lonely, or possibly not yet confident enough, to Trek their chosen path in the right direction and just wanted some entertaining company while they made up their mind.)

- **True or False: *The deeper the RUT you travel, the more effort is required to continue the Trek.*** (*Absolutely True!* Either when traveling a well-worn path or as a Trekker approaches the end of a chosen RUT, great faith is needed to maintain and manage the original purpose of the journey. If I invite in the Trekkers who answer *False*, the more likely I'll be dragging them out of, or leaving them in a PIT Stop somewhere along the way.)

---

[53] Oooooo, Ahhhhh!

- **True or False:** *You usually don't know you're in a RUT until you're in a RUT.* I really don't care how they answer this one because, whether or not they realize—unless they're a Blazer[54]—THEY'RE IN A RUT. I just like to watch people's facial expressions as they try to fit this question properly within their cortex, especially those from California..."You mean, I wouldn't like, you know...really know...like until I knew...or would it be like, not even knowing that I didn't know...like...say...what's a RUT again?"

By the way, I can only speak for myself in the realm of RUTology. I'm just as liable to be excluded on someone's "RUT Trek Preferred Companion List," and I'm capable of handling such rejection. NASA, me, or any of us must carefully choose our RUT partners because we don't want to have to spend a lot of time in outer space cooped up in a RUT space capsule managing our relationships, when the true focus should be the journey to the stars!

Moving ahead: Upon defining their RUT, "NASAlites"..."NASAnians"...the GEEKS would then have to ask themselves:

Have I properly mapped my RUT?

And how does mapping differ from defining? Fair enough, I'll respond with the answer in question: When I decide to take a vacation and I pick the location, say for instance The Fur and

---

[54] I'll know whether or not they're a Trail Blazer because they'll get all indignant and snooty, holding their hands dramatically up to their chest and saying something like "I've never been in a RUT in my entire life!" Which is, of course, a lie, but there's no use telling Blazers that. Anyway, don't bother inviting them along; they'll say "No."

Feathers Rainforest Tree House in North Queensland,[55]; just because I know my preferred destination (i.e. the definition of my vacation choice) does that mean I know how to get there?

Mapping the predicted course of my RUT involves internally "imaging" the place where I want to arrive and then…getting directions. This involves seeking out others who have been there before, possibly even Trail Blazers, and finding out how they got there. Is it that simple? If I map it, will that insure a well defined Trek? RUT-Blocks and detours are a product of any journey. Why?

- **RUT Rule Number Twenty-three**: *A RUT, is a RUT, is a RUT, is a…*[56]

At some point, after getting all the directions my little brain can handle, and then thinking about, and sweating about, and praying about…and whatever else I do about…I have to finally decide to jump into my chosen RUT to get to my internally "imaged" destination. Oh yes, the RUT already exists. Remember, *I didn't create my RUT. There was at least one Trail Blazer who got to the Fur and Feathers first!* From this point forward it's all about deciding when to stay on course, or when to Re-RUT to assure I reach my ultimate destination.

RUT to the Point

In deference to NASA, it doesn't take a Rocket Scientist to plan a RUT Trek. In deference to RUT Trekkers, most of you

---

[55] Of course it exists, why would I invent such a thing? Reference found at www.unusualhotelsoftheworld.com/ HotelDetails.aspx?HotelID=355&sender=map&cid=9

[56] You get the idea.

never take the time to do what the NASA geeks did so well and so simply. That is:

Before jumping into the RUT with both feet, step back and make sure that it's the right RUT, with the right Trekkers, with the right directions.

It all sounds rudimentary, but the evidence still argues that, since we're so easily tempted off track, we've got to lay out a plan…and follow it if we ever want to get where we originally planned to get!

GET it?

CHAPTER SIX

The RUT Challenge
Completing the Trek from Reliance to Revelation

Always looking to the future—this one—
Never his mind on where he was, what he was doing!
—Yoda

Most people know the story of Martin Luther, the great reformation theologian who broke out of the mold of the Catholic Church to help make the reading/understanding of the Bible and the open discussion of theological beliefs, a right of the *common* man. Here was a man who forged ahead, taking a bold and risky stand, fighting against the authority of the time and speaking out as his own man, right? Wrong!

Luther was certainly and ultimately a proponent of the new reformed church, but it's revealing to look at his early life and his statements about the Church before labeling him completely.

Brought up in a wealthy family, Martin attended a prestigious school intending to become a prominent lawyer. But the man's ultimate chosen profession was that of monk! In case that's a foreign concept to you, envision hours upon hours of prayer and isolation, intermittent with vows of silence and a lifetime commitment to poverty, days on days of devotional study; years buried within years[57] of unceasing discipline and submission to

---

[57] Ten years in Martin's case

God. Was this the lifestyle of a Trail Blazer? I think not. It wasn't until the leaders of the day started abusing their power to gather wealth for the Church, that Luther discovered a sense of discontent. It took a remarkable and courageous effort on his part to break out of the old ways and forge a new road that would help change the world.[58]

And isn't that the way of history? I tend to view certain successful people as my heroes, and I'm prone to assume that they became successful by being radically different, when reality actually points out that, most hysterical[59] figures are not the rebels they appear to be in retrospect. In fact, most acknowledged achievers got that way by methodically and incessantly following a pre-set course—even in the face of great adversity, criticism, and turmoil. Translated?

▸ **RUT Rule Number Twenty-four:** *No matter "where," it's Your RUT that will get you "there".*

I've got the mind-set. I have the internal image. I know the plan and the people. So, now 'it's time' for me to jump in and start RUTting. Everything seems to be going swimmingly, everybody's happy, when suddenly there's a hard turn in the RUT. Someone or something stands in the way and says, "There will be some delays up ahead that require a whole lot more work on you're part," or, "The RUT will be very, VERY boring for the next part of the Trek and we're not sure when it will get un-boring." What do I do? Well of course, I jump off! After all, who wants to hang around when things aren't easy and interesting? That's just not the way of things. OK, OK, I might hang around a little bit, but I'll complain a lot. Maybe I'll Back-Trek and check

---

[58] Luther historical references found at http://www.educ.msu.edu/homepages/laurence/reformation/Luther/Luther.htm

[59] Maybe it's supposed to be "historical," I believe I spelled that wrong, but I'm going to leave it that way, because *I can*!

in with RUT Trekkers who are following me. I might even warn them that there's a glitch ahead. Who knows, they might want to stop in their tracks and form a PIT because the place where they are seems real nice. But me? Ultimately, I want to get where I've decided to go and if this RUT won't take me there, I will FIND another way!

And so begins the sad tale of wasted time and effort, of costly ventures ill-defined that lead no where near where I really want to be. Why? Because I wasn't willing to stick to the RUT Plan!

If only I were able to follow the path Luther followed, or take the RUT Teddy Roosevelt or Clara Barton Trekked, those were interesting RUTs...but those were *their* RUTs, not mine. And along the way, I suspect they too, encountered problems or slowdowns enticing them closer towards the "fishhook" of Re-RUTting in the middle of a perfectly good RUT Trek. The difference between them and me? They didn't take the bait!

How do I overcome the temptation to veer off and start Trekking a different RUT? Wait a minute, I'm confused, what if the RUT I want to jump out of really wasn't the right one for me and now really *is* the time to Re-RUT? How do I figure these things out?

▸ **RUT Rule Number Twenty-five:** *When a choice of RUTs is presented, a choice must be made.*

Notice I didn't say that we should go searching for RUTs to follow. There are plenty out there, but they don't all connect. And if they don't connect in some way, they won't get you to the place where you originally wanted to arrive.

Crucial point here—the cows you see in a pasture sticking their heads through the barbed wire to get to the greener grass are still lodged solidly on their side of the fence. It's a fool's paradise thinking you can Trek in one RUT while exploring another. MAKE A CHOICE! Where's your destination? Which way do you go? *PITs are the camp of the undecided.* But the question still stands—What do I need to do to *"best choose"* between *best* RUT *paths?*

RUT Comparisons

The only way I've discovered to understand the value of my existing RUT, compared to a new path option, is to do a little Back-RUTting. I basically start by taking a quick look back over my shoulder and ask a very basic question:

> ***Is my original RUT acceptable to me in the direction it leads me?***

I've got to answer that before heading off in any other direction, because the hard truth is:

> ***If my RUT is going to get me where I want to go, even if it's not as sexy or maneuverable as I thought it would be, then I'd spend a lot less time and arrive a whole lot more quickly if I simply stayed the course rather than investing in the quest of another route.***

Now, as a renowned RUTologist, I have a few tools in my RUT-Pack to help in my excavation of the answer. And as a follower of RUTology,[60] you too can make use of these tools. Remember in Chapter Three when we discussed the "stair-step" pattern of Reliance, supporting Relevance, creating Realization, leading to Revelation? Well, now it's time to put the pattern to work.

---

[60] No, you've not been initiated into some strange cult. RUTs are the way of life and you are living (I hope). Therefore, you are a student of life's RUTs. Can we move on now?

Reliance

Each of these four RUT factors correlates to the others, but the Trek starts here. Without a reliable basis for my belief in where I'm going and what I'm doing, I'm going to be much more prone to abandoning ship. So, whether deciding to jump into a RUT, or just want to remind myself of why I chose the path I'm already on, I have to make sure that it's dependable. How do I measure RUT dependability? It's all about people, places, and things:

Mark's RUT Reliance Register

- Look to see who's in the RUT—*can I depend on them and they on me?*

- Look to see where the RUT is going—*can I depend on it to get me where I want to go?*

- Look at the things that are in the RUT (duties and actions required along the Trek)—**are those things I can depend on to help me get where I'm going?**

Well, what's so new and provocative about those three questions, you ask? Any idiot can do that, you say! Yes, but my pride tells me I'm smarter than an idiot.[61] The question is: *Am I smart enough to be humble enough to RUT like an idiot?*

If I set up my reliance paradigm in the right way and ask the questions honestly of myself, it will be easy to go back and assess its dependability. It also allows me to predict the same for any new RUT I might be tempted by. And I'll be a better RUT

---

[61] Don't you be goin' there!

partner for everyone involved. Oh yes, it *does* mean I have to open my eyes and really LOOK both ways up and down my RUT!

Relevance

In the course of evaluating which RUT is mine, I really have to be asking, "What can that power do for me and every one else involved in my RUT?" Going back to the car analogy, it's what makes me move and what keeps me going. It's my "RUT Wheels."

When I have momentum, it's difficult not to accomplish something along the RUT path. The problem lies in when I stop the RUT Trek—when I either encounter an obstacle, or I simply grow weary and put the car in "park" at a rest stop—I am at risk.

Indecision Pauses Purpose.

That's why it's vital to stop only long enough to get my bearings, or to make the switch to another RUT. How do I make sure I don't loose my original faith? I can't. I *will* doubt, that's part of any RUT Trek. But here's the catch…

Doubt isn't the evil twin sister to faith, but its parent.

I can't be motivated to move unless I fear the unknown right where I am. The key is to be less afraid of the unknown ahead. It's better—it has to be—that's what my FAITH tells me. Here's how I use my doubt and my faith to make the decision to continue on the current RUT Trek or jump to another:

Mark's RUT Relevance Register

- List what you've learned in the Trekking of Your RUT (ALL OF IT; even the small things)—*Is the learning process still helping[62] you get closer to you're chosen destination?*

- List what you've accomplished in the Trekking of Your RUT (ALL OF IT, *even the small things)—Are your accomplishments relevant to helping you reach your chosen destination?*

- List the feedback of fellow RUT Trekkers (ALL OF IT; blah, blah, blah)—*Do they think you're still on the right track leading to your chosen destination?*

Listing is a difficult concept because once down on paper, a thought, feeling, or belief becomes remarkably tangible. It's a critical step of commitment and that's where I am headed with this whole exercise. If you find that your document is an outline of exactly what you had imagined doing when you started your journey, then TREK ON HARD and don't look back! If you can't identify what you've learned that is still relevant to your Trek, how you've contributed to the journey, or what your value is to others in the same RUT (You'll discover this through their comments, not by your own internal examination and self-criticism), then another RUT might be waiting for you.

▸ **RUT Rule Number Twenty-six:** *RUTs require management along the entire Trek.*

---

[62] "Helping"—a complex term that means "Being Relevant" (Excuse the sarcasm—it's a part of the RUT I'm in).

Realization

This is so much fun…no, REALLY! You see, this book is a primary example of how my RUT success is measured and should serve as a great illustration for you, too. I've shared with you how I love writing, and that enjoyment prompted me to try to find a way to share an idea with others that would be universal and yet unique. But that Trek started years ago and involved nothing regarding RUTs or Management or Healthy Male Deer or really anything specific. Still, I started on a journey and this is where it has taken me. Somewhere a couple of turns back, I came close to beginning a book, but ran up against a RUT-Block that suggested I was on the wrong Trek all together…VERY FRUSTRATING.

I started second guessing myself and doubting my convictions. So I looked back at where I had come from, re-examined the image of what I thought I was trying to attain, researched my notes, sat down with some friends who shared my passion for the pen, and listened to their wise council…. IS ANY OF THIS CONNECTING WITH YOU? It was the very process of RUT Management that I've outlined in this chapter that I used to test my own RUT. Ironically, the RUT idea was an "aside" project I had shelved a while back and when one of my cohorts asked, "What else have you considered writing about?" Voila! The corner was turned and my same reliable RUT continues onward.

Did the work I had to do then—research, create an actual book outline and final product—bring me closer to the end of my RUT? You bet. Actually, I started Trekking so fast once I got around the barrier, that I felt more empowered and freer to follow my RUT than ever before. By writing this book, have I finished my RUT? No way! So I continue on. Will I run into other RUT-Blocks? Is water wet?

What I'm getting at is that Realization happens without much testing involved. It's a result…correction…it's a *reward* received from faithfully Relying on a Relevant RUT plan. Some of you might ask, "What if I discover that I'm not getting what I expected out of my RUT and it's not leading me where I want and everyone is telling me so? This is not feeling very good!"

When did I say RUT Realization has to feel good? Did I mention that? Class? Anyone? Here's a bit-o-RUT Wisdom I want you to memorize:

> *RUT Realization can be incredibly uplifting or dismally disappointing, but its result is the greatest reward ANY RUT can offer.*

You don't get it, you say? Understandable, who wants to go through the hassle and pain of changing course when you've thrown all that time and energy into your long term RUT? But that's the great thing about it. If properly planned and managed, your RUT is never wasted:

▸ **RUT Rule Number Twenty-seven:** *The better I do at setting up my RUT, the better I'll do at deciding if my RUT needs to be changed.*

Now, as far as a Realization Register is concerned, it's pretty simple:

Mark's Realization Register

■ **Learn from my RUT: Why is it a good Trek or a bad Trek to travel?**

One question only, not three as in the other registers. And notice there's no "Middle-Of-The-RUT" here. I have all the information available that I need to decide if I'm satisfied with my

RUT. And if I'm not, I'd better Back-RUT to the Relevance Stage to find out why not,[63] before determining what to do about it!

Revelation

Talk to anyone who's had one. No, actually observe anyone who's experiencing one. They are truly weird. You can just tell by their actions and behavior that they would not want to be Trekking in any other path except for where they are. They don't need to be asked to do things, because doing things is what they're all about. They usually are followed by others who want to get things done because they're usually creating more new things to do than they can possibly accomplish. They've got that peculiar "far off" look in their eyes that says "WOW," even on the rainiest and gloomiest of days. Energy? Let's talk "nuclear." There are not enough hours on the clock for a Revelationist when they've been charged with a mission. All of this and more…while still stuck in a RUT. Imagine that.

You can recognize RUT Trekkers who have experienced Revelation because they are DRIVEN. Maybe a better description would be, THEY ARE DRIVING…themselves, their relationships and everything they're about. If you see one coming up from behind you, start moving faster or get out of the way. You will not stop them; they will not be hindered. What is it about someone endowed with RUT Revelation that is so different (Well, besides the fact that they've successfully navigated Reliance and Relevance, thus achieving Realization and now possessing an overwhelming and self-consuming belief that they've actually seen

---

[63] Caution: This isn't an emotional decision. We're not talking "happy" or "sad" here, but a literal REALIZATION that "I'm doing what I said I wanted to be doing." Don't let emotions cloud the Trek; you'll end up bumping into an unnecessary RUT wall or two.

the end of their RUT before it ever appears on the horizon?)? And they absolutely, without doubt, have a mental and spiritual beacon now indelibly lodged somewhere inside that won't switch off which guides them on? Besides those things? Nothing, really.

Revelation is the easiest of all to measure and evaluate. You either have one or ya don't. The "Dos" know it. The "Don'ts" know it—no making this stuff up.[64] Management, not measurement, is the slippery slope of Revelation. Let's face it, Revelation is exciting and romantic. It's very tempting to let the emotion of it sweep you off your feet. But how do I live with my RUT Revelation after the honeymoon? There are things I'd better know about my true love before settling in for the long haul.

Revelations come in two flavors: *Indescribably Wonderful* and *Describably Terrifying* (Everybody thinks they want to only experience the former, but oddly, just as many of the best Revelations are of the *Terrifying* type, the kind that scare the RUT Revelationist out of deep sleep, sweating and suddenly craving a mother figure to cling to, wanting badly to bestow the honor of receiving said prophecy upon some other lucky soul.). It really doesn't matter:

▸ **RUT Rule Number Twenty Eight:** *We don't get to choose our RUT Revelations; our Trek chooses them for us.*

The question is, "What do I do, once chosen by my Revelation?" It's hard to contain a Revelation and that's the greatest challenge to the RUT Trek. Revelation wants to keep jumping out of the box. Fine, I say, let it JUMP, because there is

---

[64] But ironically, Revelation descriptions sound much like passages out of the Bible or from some mystery novel written by a certain popular writer who resides in the state of Maine.

no relation between the six sides of a box and the path of a RUT.[65]

All this said, human nature tends to relate RUTs to boxes (remember our pastor friend?), suggesting that creative inspiration and unbounded spirit cannot exist in a RUT. Let me assure you *they can and do.* You might observe that RUT Revelationist traits sound strangely like those of a Trail Blazer. Interesting you should think that. The Trekker who receives Revelation in a RUT may end up becoming a Trail Blazer. Breaking off to forge new territory is an option that a lot of Revelationists choose. RUT Management suggests this happens way too often and that the better solution is to stay IN the RUT to forge a stronger, not a different, path to complete.

> *The dare with Revelation is having the patience to run it out—in a RUT.*

Speaking of how to decide whether to keep the Revelation in the RUT or head out on the undiscovered trail—that very critical decision requires me to cling tenaciously to the simplest RUT Rule of All.

▸ **RUT Rule Number Twenty-nine:** *Remember Relationship.*

Sounds easy, but there's an inherent conflict between Individual Revelation and RUT Relationship, and it goes back to the fact that Revelation comes to me, not the other way around. Once I'm "smitten," I become a jealous lover. My Revelation is THE REVELATION...*THE ONLY REVELATION*...EVER! I'll share it, but everyone else MUST understand that what I have

---

[65] Now the similarities between a PIT and a Box are an entirely different matter. See my book, "PIT Bull" (not to be confused with that fabulous Texas invention, the Barbeque PIT)

received is the most earth shattering manifestation ever imagined. Here's **Revealing Point Number One**:

> *If I can't get beyond the belief that mine is the ONLY Revelation, I will become a Trail Blazer—I'll have to because no one else will tolerate my company.*

Interesting isn't it, that most RUT Revelationists' and Trail Blazers' destinies are so defined by the companions they're able to—or not able to—gather to their cause?

Now comes the real work for the successful RUT Revelationists. Once they decide to stick to the RUTted Trek, sharing their "Grand Prize" with the marching masses, they need to realize and accept **Revealing Point Number Two**:

> *Other people Trekking the same RUT with me can have different revelations.*

That's the funny thing about Revelation; even if I accept that other Trekkers can receive Revelation, I expect them to have had the same Revelation I've had, and to have had it at the very same time. Not only that, but then I expect everyone to start moving at exactly the same pace I am now moving.[66] Truth: It's simply not true, and the sooner a RUT Revelationist figures this out, the smoother the rest of the journey will go TOGETHER. By the way, accepting this also weeds out any straggling Trail Blazers improving the communal RUT Trek significantly.

---

[66] Which is of course "high speed" because I've just received a RUT Revelation so I'm very animated and full of caffeine because I drink LOTS OF COFFEE when that happens

One final Revealing Point[67]:

Some people are NOT experiencing, nor have they EVER before experienced, nor might they in the future experience any Revelational RUT moments.

They have no clue as to why the Revelationist is frothing at the mouth; as a matter of fact, it scares them to watch it occurring in other Trekkers. Love them and try to swallow more to keep your "foam factor" down. They are true and faithful followers who serve to succeed, and so succeed to serve. They, not the Revelationist, are the very foundation of any RUT and so should be treasured, not tolerated.[68]

RUT to the Point

And that's the dance. We all experience challenges in the different stages of RUT Trekking—just not at the same time:

The ability to recognize where you are in your individual RUT process and then manage your individual Trek rather than trying to change everyone else's RUT to match yours: THAT's the dividing difference between RUT rapid transit and bumper cars!

---

[67] That would be RP #3.

[68] Sermon over; soapbox safely stored away.

CHAPTER SEVEN

A Tale of Two RUTs

No man is born either naturally or supernaturally with character; he has to make character. Nor are we born with habits; we have to form habits on the basis of the new life God has put into us. We are not meant to be illuminated versions, but the common stuff of ordinary life exhibiting the marvel of the grace of God. Drudgery is the touchstone of character. The great hindrance in spiritual life is that we will look for big things to do. "Jesus took a towel...and began to wash the disciples' feet."
—Oswald Chambers

What about "Those Days"?

You know the ones I'm talking about...yeah, THOSE days...when I'm weary in every fiber of my body from following a path I'm not sure is correct, and I'm screaming to myself, "Self... Escape!"? About now you're wondering, "This nut case has taken six chapters and hours out of my life to preach the upside of RUTs and NOW he's saying they can cause problems?" Yes, you may start shooting at any time...but if you do, you'll miss the biggest and most fundamental point that RUT Management offers.

Even if you do everything recommended in the last six chapters, at one time or another, you will feel, as I have that, "This is the moment to Re-RUT or become a Trail Blazer, because nothing's working, no one's cooperating, my RUT's going the wrong direction, or no direction at all." And thus, the Question De Jour becomes not, *"When do I choose?"* or even **"Where do I choose to go?"** but rather, *"What am I choosing?"* There are two ways to go when it comes to RUTting. One way is to look at the timing issues of my RUT Trekking (We've hammered that method to death in previous chapters!). Now it's time to look at another perspective of RUTs by *trenching-in* to make the really tough decision. Ask yourself:

Do I manage my RUT, or do I let my RUT manage me?

And suddenly you're confused. Of course you would choose to manage your RUT. Of course you've taken the wisdom of these pages to heart and OF COURSE nothing would stand in the way of that choice…but what about THOSE days? The BAD days? If I'm managing my RUT with precision and panache, shouldn't THOSE days just cease to be, vaporized in a puff of smoke by the very aura of my RUT confidence? A simple truth:

> *The quality of your RUT Management will have little, if any, impact on the amount of crap that comes your way. It does however directly affect the outcome of how you deal with the crap.*[69]

Whether it's a day of "good stuff" or "bad stuff" coming my way, it's still a day on my path preference. But to tell myself just to step over the refuse lying before me on my RUT path is treating the magnitude of such obstacles far too lightly. It involves time and effort…and it smells…and it's messy, and…it can sting, even hurt…A LOT.

---

[69] Let me apologize now for the crappy vernacular, there's just no better word for me to describe it. There are probably better words you can come up with. Feel free to substitute.

My temptation? Well gee, that's easy: If it's painful and un-fun and the road is blocked and...when it's become a RUT just to follow my RUT, then I must jump to another RUT, **right**? But then again, if I'm using the measurement methods from Chapter Six, I'll overcome my initial doubts and Trek right on over all the...minutia, demonstrating once again that I will not be teased into a PIT Stop...**right**? Wait a moment. Perhaps, just maybe, neither option offers the answer I'm looking for and I'll decide to break out completely into Trail Blazing Territory—*RUT be damned*, **right**?

Let's see. By my count, that makes three **rights** and if I'm headed forward in my RUT, and then take three rights...I end up **right** back where I started...*right*? Yes, I'm talking in circles, because sometimes, RUTs *do* run that way, even though we've done everything **right**. AND I...excuse me...WE DON'T LIKE TO TREK IN CIRCLES. It's that "human nature thing" again; something about progress being measured in "forward motion," or "sticking to the straight and narrow," or "climbing the ladder of success," or "me taking the high road and getting to Scotland afore you," or some such drivel. Watch out! Here comes some wisdom on this matter:

Delays, Detours, and BackRUTs are not always things to overcome quickly; they allow the Trek to be purposely slowed down.

"Slowed down? For what purpose Mark?"

I don't know! And besides, you're focusing on the wrong words. The "purpose" is something *you* need to discover, not me. I know my purpose, which right now is to bring your attention to the speed-factor involved in RUT Trekking—hence an emphasis on the words "Slowed Down."[70] Unlike Revelation, which always kicks the Trek into overdrive, allowing very little time to think, the RUT Slowdown invites introspection and a centering-in on the "why" of things, rather than on the tasks-at-hand. That's the problem...

▸ **RUT Rule Number Thirty:** *When the RUT Trek slows down, do not mistake the reduction in momentum as a signal for immediate Re-RUTting!*

It's in the quagmire of the RUT Slow-Down that the metal of the Trekker is *Trench-Tested*. It's the best time for me to effectively review the first three RUT Steps...

...Looking to see if my RUT is still a Reliable Path;

...Listing its Relevance to the purpose I originally set out to accomplish, and then;

...Learning from my results to see if I can still Realize the full potential of my RUT.

Am I saying that you should never veer off course, changing from one RUT to another? You haven't been listening very well have you? At certain times I'm designed to follow the trail methodically and purposefully; at other times I'm to *break-out*. But knowing first why, and then how, where, and finally when any of

---

[70] As in "Reduced Momentum" which suggests an intentional braking before I slam into the Trekker in front of me—a good idea even if I were to have RUT collision insurance...which to my knowledge isn't available on the open market yet. "Reduced Momentum" is not to be confused with "Spinning My Wheels" which implies going nowhere fast and burning unnecessary RUT Rubber prior to an uncontrolled acceleration, impressing no one.

these determined actions are to be taken, is what the RUT Slow-Down allows for.

Before the Re-RUT

Obviously, I'm presenting the idea that ReRUTting should be a carefully thought out process. Think about it. Changing habits and RUTines and systems and processes and all of the things that maintain RUT Momentum takes a lot of energy. YOUR Energy.[71] Having tried to switch RUTs, I can assure you, it's not all it's cracked up to be, mostly because the challenges associated with following RUTs, are pretty much universal, meaning...

▸ **RUT Rule Number Thirty-one:** *Swapping RUTs alters the destination, not the RUT Rules.*

Saying that and having given you copious ways to evaluate your RUT to determine if it's the right way to keep Trekking, you may still hear a little voice in your brain saying, "This Trek is hard, this Trek is VERY hard" and the other little voice responding, "Is it too hard?" Before checking into a local mental health establishment, know this:

If you're not having conversations with yourself about the difficulty of holding true to your Trek, your RUT is worthless.

---

[71] Just the task of FINDING the energy necessary can be daunting. People spend huge amounts of money on aerobics and gym memberships toward this very objective. Other people resort to mass infusions of chocolate. I confess to trying both. The Chocolate RUT-Energy program is preferable.

That's right. Any truly good RUT requires not just patience, but sweat, toil, and even anguish. Interesting that most of us say we want "out" of our RUTs because of the implied monotony. I argue that, if I'm honest with myself, I'm more prone to jump RUTs because of the hard choices I'm required to make, rather than the mundane actions I perform every day in order to maintain my Trek. This requires an extra step in order to avoid making an emotional, rather than an informed choice, regarding the RUT in which you find yourself so heavily invested.

That step is to know your enemy. Yes, you have one; it's called *RUT Frustration.* And to know your enemy, you need to listen in to your enemy's conversations. And to do that, you need to know the "Secret Enemy RUT Code Language."[72] Here are the signals that you'll most likely pick up, which should warn you that a "battle of the mind and spirit" is about to take place:

RUT Frustration Signals

- There's a RUTine in my life that I want to drop-kick off the edge of the earth.
- There is a specific part of my RUT that I can name which "gets me down" more than anything else.
- I feel like I'm "scraping bottom" and I'm not "on my game."
- I keep telling myself "I like it where I am," when I know I don't.

The *RUT Frustration Factor* nags at each of us, compelling each person to change just for the sake of "Uncomfortableness." The successful Trekker recognizes this and knows to use the RUT Slowdown as a normal road sign indicating current road

---

[72] Where will you hear these strange little conversations? In a quite place, alone, with only yourself for company; trust me, a padded room is not required; this is a GOOD place to be.

conditions, rather than as detour barriers demanding a change of course.

So, let's say I've experienced a Slowdown, gone through my Trench Testing, identified some RUT Frustration Signals, and reviewed all of my RUT Steps; this is when I REALLY start to get impatient. Now I actually see how much work staying In-RUT involves and I'm ready to give it all up for the chance to seek another route to my destiny…this is the critical RUT moment to remember a very important rule:

▸ **RUT Rule Number Thirty-two:** *The point of breaking out of a RUT is only to forge a new RUT.*

Again, back to the energy thing; whether you're in one RUT or move to another, the rules and the effort remain the same. And this is where I let you in on a dirty little secret…

…RUTs can be dirty places.

That's right. When I'm Trekking, truly Trekking, I'm liable to bump into a wall or two. I'm subject to all of the elements and environment that surround me. My RUT is not a protected place, just a predictable one. And you know what? Getting dirty is healthy! It means I'm *interacting*, not just *observing*, and it's probably the best indicator of all that I'm in touch with my RUT Relationships.

The Unwanted RUT

Where was I? Oh yes, THOSE days…and…what about "Those Weeks and "Those Months" and even "Those Years" when you just don't like your RUT? Maybe the better term would be, "HATE your RUT," but you know of no place to escape to?

A RUT path involves good and bad experiences. Not only that, just because my RUT is predictable, it doesn't mean I can see all of the answers to the challenges before me. Even the RUT Revelationist has for inspiration, at best, an incomplete map. This is when I want to encourage all RUT Trekkers with a real life story about how challenging, yet rewarding, sticking to your chosen RUT path can be, even when the future seems very murky and unpleasant. Before I go on though, I want to warn you; I'm about to get serious... Real Serious...there will be no footnotes in this next section... Really.

One of the most compelling examples of RUT Management I know comes not from the archives of the great and famous, nor from some ancient writings of the wise and righteous. It's a contemporary lesson given to me by a friend, Scott and his wife Pam.

This experience started several years back when Scott (a business relation whom I'd come to respect for many reasons) and I started sharing our journals. It was a "spiritual thing;" part of our mutual RUTs that I won't detail now because it bears no significance to the story, other than through the process of sharing, we began risking a great deal by chipping away at the social barriers and thus, laying bare our personal space. We became... *Trek Partners.*

Sometime within this RUT Ritual, our mutual Trek kicked up a notch as Scott revealed that his wife Pam had been diagnosed with a rare form of Lymphoma and that extensive treatment was necessary. There was the usual request for prayers of healing and for words of encouragement, but Scott took this part of his RUT far more seriously than I anticipated. He began an almost daily report of his interactions with, observations of, and reactions to Pam's experience. He chronicled her trips to the hospital, her chemo-therapy reactions, their discussions about treatment, and as importantly, the daily opportunities they passionately sought after to keep their relationship fresh and alive. Pam continued to cook and entertain and shop and travel when she was not confined to a hospital bed. Many other journal followers and I were direct observers of Pam's struggles and joys through the loving eyes of Scott. This became a very intimate RUT that suddenly did not involve an individual journey, but more of an exodus of shared experience and emotion.

Through this man's devotion, we privileged Trekkers marched side-by-side with Pam through weeks and months and years of turmoil. Mornings of triumph and dark nights of frustration consistently poured out of Scott's words as he detailed the doctors, caregivers, family, and the couple's struggle to understand and live within the "day-to-day" of Pam's course. Scott never faltered in his dogged pursuit of sharing love and giving care, even as this extremely energy-consuming RUT continued to wear on.

And then, a little more than a year after the vigil began, I received an e-mail from Scott unlike all others. He announced that the doctors had stopped all treatment and that there was nothing more medically that could be done, other than to make Pam comfortable. But Scott, exhausted to his very fiber, still would not give up his responsibility within their kindred RUT, remaining diligent to his cause and painfully open in his reporting. As with each and every journal entry before, he wrote this request…"We are still praying for a miracle for her. Please continue to persistently pray for Pam."

Persistence defined this husband and wife over the next weeks: Pam receiving visits from close friends and relatives, and Scott, ever vigilant, responding to her needs, her increasing pain, and her inevitable decline. How do I know? Because even then, he continued to share with us, his journal entries, not allowing fear or grief to stave off the desire to allow others a share in the wonder of this Trek.

Pam died with a dignity that few of us can imagine. Not just because of the special inner strength bestowed to her and spiritual faith, which she professed and lived out to the last moment; but because she and Scott refused to be alone on her earthly Trek. Her RUT willingly became Scott's RUT, and by his catharsis, I too traveled the hard miles with them. No, I did not die, and no,

I did not lose my bride; yet a part of me did lose…and another part of me gained something deeper within my own RUT as I learned to pray persistently…for Pam and for Scott, and for those I love.

RUT to the Point

And so, Pam and Scott have both reached the end of a RUT; both to begin new, but this time separate adventures. You won't see the total message revealed in the words of this illustration as I can't adequately paint the picture of the endurance and the courage and the blind faith that were all required parts of their (and our) time together. I hope this inspiring example will surface one day from some place far back in your brain as the most powerful of RUT Lessons, reminding you, as it continues to remind me…

…Whether your RUT experience is entirely wonderful, or as in Pam and Scott's case, includes a rollercoaster ride ending in grueling loss, at the very end of each RUT hides an amazing treasure called **Completion**. It's why I offer this book: *To help all RUT Trekkers, no matter where we are in our journeys, and no matter how taxing our previous experiences, to stop perceiving the RUTine, the structure, and the difficult steps of life as unromantic or disenchanting ordeals.*

And what about Scott now? He continues to Trek on in a new RUT, for his new life shaped and sharpened by the love and devotion he faithfully measured out in each step he took with Pam. The message is simple:

▸ **RUT Rule Number Thirty-three:** *Don't be easily enticed away from life's discipline only for the sake of change. The flowers and the thorns encountered in the landscape of our RUT Paths should be considered precious gifts to guide us all to the completion of our journeys.*
Thank you Pam and Scott.

CHAPTER EIGHT

Arrival!

THE ROAD NOT TAKEN

Two roads diverged in a yellow wood,
And sorry I could not travel both
And be one traveler, long I stood
And looked down one as far as I could
To where it bent in the undergrowth;
Then took the other, as just as fair,
And having perhaps the better claim,
Because it was grassy and wanted wear;
Though as for that the passing there
Had worn them really about the same,
And both that morning equally lay
In leaves no step had trodden black.
Oh, I kept the first for another day!
Yet knowing how way leads on to way,
I doubted if I should ever come back.
I shall be telling this with a sigh
Somewhere ages and ages hence:
Two roads diverged in a wood, and I-
I took the one less traveled by,
And that has made all the difference
—Robert Frost

Know what? At first blush, the content of Bobby's[73] old rune suggests that I'm full of that stuff from Texas...what was it called again? Bum Steer? Maybe it was some other term that had to do with just a portion of the bovine...anyway...I come to you now with a new consideration. What if something you've always thought to be true...wasn't? What if the assertion that the majority of the RUTting population of this planet are prone to not follow a RUT all the way to completion? What if the Real Entrepreneur is not the Trail Blazer, but instead, the RUT Trekker who actually follows through all the way on a commitment and makes it to the very end of his or her RUT?

Is that such a difficult idea to swallow? History is full of examples of real RUT heroes; I've mentioned several in the book. But the one I started with, who sets the standard for RUT completion, is none other than Moses: His history illustrates the RUT of all RUTs. You know the guy:

> Born on the wrong side of the tracks, to the wrong family in the wrong culture, Moses is given a unique chance to live out a RUT of luxury and great influence as an adopted son of the most powerful ruler of that time. Then came...a Revelation; but this Revelation is unusual because it suggests Moses is in the wrong RUT.
>
> He decides to make the leap,[74] taking on a cause no one else would dare consider—leading a bunch

---

[73] I can call him Bobby, you know. It's OK, because I'm a writer too, and we writers hang out at cafés together smoking cheroots and are on a "nickname" basis. Anyway, Bobby is "bones" now and I suspect doesn't care much what I call him. Oh by the way, I hate smoking, especially cheap French cigarettes.

[74] Well, maybe not a leap; more like a snail-crawl as it took Moses 40 years to decide to give up his old gig, then another 40 years in a tent out in the country to figure out what God was telling him to do. But once that burning bush lit up, I bet Moses leapt...at least 40 feet.

of slaves on a Trek out of a country that doesn't want them to leave—into another country inhabited by people who don't want the slaves to come in. All the while, the slaves are whining and God is thinking about zapping the slaves because they're so whiny, and Moses has to decide if he has the chutzpah to keep everyone from killing each other before they get to their new home.

The slaves finally "tick" God off so badly, that He tells Moses to make them do "laps" in the wilderness for another forty years—a number God seems to like a lot—until all the old slaves die off. Moses, being the good and faithful Trekker he is, leads by example, and in doing so, teaches the slaves a form of discipline and theological RUT Management[75] that will define their culture, religion, and their habitat for thousands of years to come.

For all the trouble and the chaos and RUT Rebellion that was Early Day Israel, they discovered something more powerful than a country, or a dominion, or a particular leader. The deeper lesson of the Exodus story is this—*The Promised Land exists,* but you have to be:

- Ready to go to its location: No Promised Land will ever come to you.
- Ready to sacrifice to get there: All RUTs leading to the Promised Land include toll booths.
- Ready to revel in the completion of your Trek: It's as OK to celebrate arrival as it is to follow.

---

[75] I guess you could say Moses was the first RUTologist, not me. But it wouldn't be exactly true because he spoke in Hebrew so RUT Management would have come out of his mouth roughly as *yawd Taw-meed* and RUTolgy would have been *daw-rash Taw-meed.* Frankly, it's all Greek to me.

RUT Lifestyle

But do I need a history lesson to help me understand my own struggle with commitments? There's a danger in writing about RUTs. I can "Write about RUTs," but am I able to "Trek the Trek"? Impatience and an insatiable curiosity caused me to veer off course incalculable[76] times. Two marriages, multiple false starts, wrong Trek Turns and other by-products of my own RUT Wavering make me…human…*very* human. But there's good news. I've learned from my history. And in the learning, I rediscovered my course and have persisted:

> I've been taught to **Rely** on my RUT's ability to get me where I need to go. I'm certain of its **Relevance** because I can see ahead of the immediate and it excites me to know that this RUT has purpose, and that other people want to share in the purpose. Now all I have to do for my **Realization** is to "stay on course" just a while longer. This frees me to focus on the adventure of being knee-deep in a RUT **Revelation** that won't quit. All this means is:

▶ **RUT Rule Number Thirty-four:** *RUTs being followed faithfully are already completed in the mindset of the Trekker.*

What does having a mindset of RUT completion mean? What does that look like? If I have a high degree of confidence that my RUT Trek will be completed when the timing is right, then my lifestyle starts reflecting that confidence. How does that

---

[76] Speaking of Greek; what kind of a word is "incalculable"? It means "can't be counted," just like the word "countless" and you already know how that one bothers me. Often, the English language just doesn't add up!

confidence help the RUT Trekker measure progress? If I base my values on the Arrival itself, all of my actions leading up to completion become focused on where, not when, my destination exists. Here's a teaser that will help explain:

> ### *Moses never stepped foot in the Promised Land, but he didn't need to!*

He's considered the greatest of all prophets, the pinnacle of humanity's attempts to be obedient to faith in a cause. In other words, Moses's faith was the RUT he lived every day of his life. Once he was able to effectively transfer that conviction of faith to others so that it became their faith lifestyle, his journey was over. He didn't need to step one foot over the border because he had already arrived at completion. Had he listened to all the griping and let it affect his confidence in what he was being commanded to do, he would have copped a plea bargain to reduce the 40-year time sentence. He might have then rushed his gang into their new home before they had established the rock-solid belief system they would need to survive the challenges that lay ahead.[77]

RUT Results

You'd think I might have mentioned before why RUTs have been such a prominent resource for the human race over time. Simple...

---

[77] Before I forget; some of you might be thinking, "Moses sure sounds more like a Trail Blazer." Nice try, now stop thinking. Moses was an observer of standards already set forth by his religious culture that had be set aside out of desperation. All he did was recognize and follow the RUT everyone else was ignoring. Now Moses's boss, HE is a Trail Blazer!

RUTs Get Results!

For some reason, results are a popular way in our culture of deciding if an action or lifestyle is worth continuing. And as I near the completion of one RUT, I'll naturally begin taking my RUT temperature to see if I'm satisfied with the outcome of my Trek. What am I looking for? What tells me that I'm done? There is no one thing, there are seven...

The Seven RUT Senses

- **Sense of Comfort**
- **Sense of Community**
- **Sense of Confidence**
- **Sense of Familiarity and Security**
- **Sense of Learning and Internalization**
- **Sense of Productivity**
- **Sense of Spiritual Well-Being**

And strangely enough, all of these results help the Trekker to achieve the ultimate result...

Arrival!

Moses knew he had arrived, because every one of the factors listed above had been achieved. I've also had the privilege of reaching a destination by following a RUT that, at first, looked "UnTrekkable." I can't describe the experience of the "sense of arrival" to you if you've never "been there." But I can suggest that you imagine having all of the above senses combined into one. John Lennon penned a popular song of imagining there is no heaven. I'd counter that the sense of Arrival is as close as any of us will ever get to said location while still participating in the

Anatomical Respiration Process.[78] Even if you don't believe in a spiritual realm, every one of us anticipates the unknown, strives to confirm its existence, and then searches out its definition, its destination, but most importantly, its origin. Attention…

That origin is the beginning of your next RUT

Whatever you want to call IT, the origin of your RUT is not a place, nor a time, but a "something" inside that urges us by some internal trigger to…Trek. Let it be a tool to help you plan your next RUT, rather than dismiss it as an emotional tangent. When you start exploring that origin more closely, you'll find it to be the strongest compass you can possibly have for your journey forward.

By the way, I've proposed an entirely new way of viewing your RUT, but don't forget RUT Rule Number…hold on…let me look it up here…yes, RUT Rule Number Twenty-three.[79] There's no need to dwell in the importance of RUT definitions. FUN yes, but if that's all you accomplish it would be a real PIT!

If a RUT is still a RUT by any other name, then nothing has really changed other than what you now do with the "nothing" that has really changed.

What really matters is your Trek and its outcome. Chew on that for a while. Meanwhile, I'm RUTting on.

---

[78] Some of us will get a whole lot closer after termination of ARP, but that's another subject. Personally, I'm looking forward to the "Eternal RUT." Sadly, we'll have to cover that in another book. I'm running out of pages.

[79] You probably thought I was just going to "spoon feed" you and not make you look up Rut Rule Number Twenty-three, didn't you! Well, OK, but just this time…RR#23 = A RUT, is a RUT, is a RUT…etc.

I should mention here that although Re-RUTting and Arrival at RUT's-End are two distinct events, the corresponding action required as a result of either is identical. Once the choice to Re-RUT has been made and the act of switching RUTs takes place, then in effect, your former RUT has come to its end. Just as in completing a RUT, this is an act to be celebrated, not mourned. Hence:

▸ **RUT Rule Number Thirty-five:** *If a decision to Re-RUT is properly made, there should be no regret or guilt associated with the leaving of the former RUT.*

Warning, warning, DANGER…I am not abdicating the idea of RUT Hopping. That word "*properly*" means that care must be taken to not change RUTs except as a last resort.

Prophet Mark talking now: I know that, if this book ever makes it to the talking heads to be anatomized on the morning shows and by Oprah (Oh please God, let it be so), I will be typecast as the fool who says "Live the mediocre life, it's all we're meant to do." Yes, I can predict the future…Yes I'm being sarcastic, but here's the grain of truth hidden in the message:

▸ **RUT Rule number Thirty-six:** *The end of one RUT is the beginning of another.*

The RUT Best Traveled

Look at how far we've Trekked together! I bet when you opened this book you thought, "RUTs? He's selling RUTs? What a nut-case." But now we're very near the end of this particular part of our sojourn and I hope at least a few of you now understand the connection of your RUT to those of the rest of us Trekkers. If I've been able to convey how valuable your RUT Trek can become just by recognizing the fun that can be had in its management, then something pretty amazing has been accomplished. And once I arrive at a "sense" of accomplishment, I can also better prepare for my next step. And what would that be? My next well-managed RUT, silly. It's a simple matter of RUTonomics 101...

> ▸ **RUT Rule Number Thirty-seven:** *The more successful I am at completing my RUT, the more confident, efficient, and productive I'll be in preparing for and completing my next RUT.*

Preparing for the Next RUT

Whether determining that Re-RUTting is the thing to do, or if I manage to arrive at RUT completion, there's still one more question that looms ever persistent in the minds and hearts of all travelers completing one journey only to begin another. It's possibly the toughest question of all...

Where do I go from here?

This part of RUT Management requires a little alone time. Sure I want others to help me in deciding and endorsing my new Trek Path, but before that can happen I have to seek out my passions.[80] And I can't risk starting on the path if I'm either not willing or not able to Trek the course all the way through. To do that, I've got to be all about a destination that "calls me" on, no matter what gets in the way. So, here are the two questions I'll want to answer before I look to outside RUT counsel for my answer:

---

[80] For the last time, we are talking about RUT Definition #1 only.

What current issues, events, and circumstances cause me to want to "react" or "respond" more than any other?

What am I afraid will happen if I don't react or respond?

Answering these questions is critical because without passion, there will be nothing to remind me of the original intensity with which I started Trekking this particular direction. Then again, with Passion I'm lead toward a two-edged path; yes I'll be far more likely to stick to the RUT, but I'll also be far more frustrated when I experience RUT Slow-downs. Passion becomes both my RUT Lifeline and my Leash.

The strange aspect of infusing passion into my RUT is its likelihood of inspiring Revelation as a normal part of my Trek.

"RUT Normalcy"

Notice how many times in this book that words like "odd" and "strange" and "weird" are associated with the idea of RUTs? Why not? Why is it that a sense of Revelationary prophecy is always considered "out of the ordinary" and "abnormal," yet its pathway, the RUT, is commonly branded as bland and mundane and emotionless?

▸ **RUT Rule Number Thirty-eight: Don't assume a RUT is predictable and unchanging.**

If my RUT becomes mind numbingly repetitive, it's because of my approach or lack of passion, not because of the Trek itself. Unawareness, exploration, and anticipation are not (as sociologists and psych-types would have us believe) warning signals of an incomplete or chaotic culture, but instead actual byproducts of a healthy RUT Lifestyle. Without them, there would be no yearning for foresight and so the drive to continue the RUT Trek to completion would die and me along with it. In Chapter Five I had mentioned that RUT Management has nothing to do with the administration of people, but everything to do with the implementation of the Trek...

RUT Management is the ability to plan, implement, and Trek through the course of one's own RUT journey.

There is however, another term that needs to be explained, one that needs to be recognized because of its significance relating to arrival. Before I give you the word, there's one more thing you need to know about RUTs. Not only is there one who trail blazes them first, but also one who arrives at RUT's-End first; which brings me to the term...

RUT Leadership: the act of encouraging others by example to follow a specific RUT Route.

This leadership will shift between different Trekkers at different points along the path, but the results remain the same. There is a beginning, there is an end, and we are all migrating from one to the other. We are a composite of travelers and, so in marching forward, require cooperation on a mammoth scale. At times we all wonder if we are just being moved forward by the sheer force of the crowd and that there is no end, just momentum. But it simply isn't so. Another truth revealed...

Where the Trail Blazer is important, the RUT Completer is crucial, because without the Completer's example of perseverance, none of the rest of us would truly believe the Trek could be finished.

How do I know? Because I've seen others before me...*arrive*. I've researched Clara Barton and her small group's incredible accomplishments. I've lived through the exciting ups and downs of NASA as they proved the impossible could become commonplace. I've absorbed a hundred times over, the exploits of Martin Luther and of Moses and, of course, the personal Trek of my friends, Scott and Pam. There are so many others I wasn't able to wedge into these pages, who have endured incredibly RUTted lives, and by their examples, continue to inspire me to Trek-On!

Smooth Trekking

I introduced this book with an allegory about driving a car on a crowded road. One of the aspects of that story which I left out was how a seasoned commuter anticipates and knows exactly when to shift lanes, seemingly moments before the former lane of travel starts clogging up. How do they know? Radio traffic reports, past experience, familiarity of the route, road signs, and word-of-mouth all contribute. The repetitive discipline utilized by these individuals makes them appear somehow gifted with driver-intuition not bestowed upon the infrequent or inattentive traveler—who has become stuck in a traffic jam along the very same path!

The same example shows up in parents who are accused by their children of seemingly having "eyes in the back of their heads," presciently knowing what their child has, or is doing, but even what they are about to do, say, or need.

RUT Trekkers firing on all cylinders, experiencing Reliance, Relevance, Realization, and Revelation, are well-aware of this phenomenon because it is the RUT Trek as it is meant to be Trekked. Does it mean that there will not be traffic tie-ups and jams? Please, if you have to ask the question, you might as well BackRUT to Chapter One and start all over again.

▸ **RUT Rule Number Thirty-nine:** *The first Trek step forward only assures an opportunity for the next Trek step.*

That's all; nothing fancy or elegant, but taken together, the steps and those stepping, set down a very interesting footprint connecting every Trekker and every RUT. In the end, Arrival doesn't depend on any one part of the Trek, but on the entire Trek experience and so…

RUTting is all about "ALL."

The successful management of my RUT Trekking not only allows me those special moments when I'm able to out maneuver the traffic jams, but also gives me the strength to endure and overcome the BackRUTs and PITs I do encounter. Is that success all of my doing and because of my special abilities? Get a grip! Exactly my point here: I'm not the only one in the universe. If I were, no RUT would be necessary. Remember Chapter Four: RUTs are interactive; Relationship is "RUT it's all about." Even the Trail Blazer recognizes how important it is to leave a path for those Trekking behind them. How much more essential is it for me as a RUT Trekker to observe, recognize, encourage, and listen to those Trekking around me? Otherwise, I'd be very much alone in a very crowded world.

RUT to the Point

Surprise, there is no RUT to this point! You're at the end. You've Arrived! Now it's time to use the map of this book to help you wherever you are along the Trek, whether that new start involves rethinking your old RUT, Re-RUTting, or possibly Trekking into your very first well-managed RUT. Regardless, be excited right where you are. Don't let the way you or others have thought about RUTs in the past be your guide. Instead, be on the lookout for those you see already using these principles.

I've shared examples of others who have obviously understood the power of RUT Management, not just as shining lights to illuminate my point, but also to subtly encourage you to consider your own RUT Heroes and to follow their leads. Who are your RUT Heroes? They're easy to spot: They're the ones moving forward with determination and a satisfied look on their face even when everything around them looks dismal. I'll warn you; start mentioning the concept of RUT Management to them and you'll get that weird look aimed your way. Why? Because they haven't been told that what they're doing is a great thing. Even though they're content and following a predetermined path as they know they need to be, no one has explained their RUT to them and that it can be shared, and that ***RUTs Are A Good Thing!*** It'll now be your job, part of your new RUT to tell them, encourage them, even Trek along with them, so that their image of Life's march begins to match the reality before them…

▸ **RUT Rule Number Forty[81]:** *RUTs Rule!*

What a good beginning to an even greater RUT to come. Now that we're ready to Trek in separate directions, I want to give you a parting charge to carry with you, one I hope and pray will challenge you and your companions to higher paths as you continue to Trek on your well-managed RUT Adventure. It's some of the best advice I can possibly think of to give you and, if followed with serious determination, will help straighten out the most twisted and confusing of paths: To all my fellow Trekkers…

Enjoy the RUTs of your life!

---

[81] I figure if the number *"Forty"* works for God, maybe it's a good one for us too.

INDEX AND REFERENCES

RUT Quotes

I hear the word, and see the image…two evenly spaced tracks leading on to some destination determined by someone else's repeated toil. The Phoenicians, the Babylonians, even the Greeks had them. Pioneer America was famous for the Western Trails; romantic notions, symbolic for what we have condemned by a single name— "RUT."—Mark A Cornelius [Introduction]

The secret of your future is hidden in your daily routine.—Mike Murdock [Chapter One]

If you come to a fork in the road, take it.—Yogi Bera [Chapter Two]

Not everything that is faced can be changed, but nothing can be changed until it is faced.—James Baldwin [Chapter Three]

No RUT in the mind is so deep as the one that says "I am the world, the world belongs to me, all people are characters in my play."—Donald Miller [Chapter Four]

The solutions all are simple—after you have arrived at them. But they're simple only when you know already what they are.—Robert M Pirsig [Chapter Five]

Always looking to the future—this one—Never his mind on where he was, what he was doing!—Yoda [Chapter Six]

No man is born either naturally or supernaturally with character, he has to make character. Nor are we born with habits; we have to form habits on the basis of the new life God has put into us. We are not meant to be illuminated versions, but the common stuff of ordinary life exhibiting the marvel of the grace of God. Drudgery is the touchstone of character. The great hindrance in spiritual life is that we will look for big things to do. "Jesus took a towel…and began to wash the disciples' feet."—Oswald Chambers [Chapter Seven]

THE ROAD NOT TAKEN
Two roads diverged in a yellow wood,
And sorry I could not travel both
And be one traveler, long I stood
And looked down one as far as I could
To where it bent in the undergrowth;
Then took the other, as just as fair,
And having perhaps the better claim,
Because it was grassy and wanted wear;
Though as for that the passing there
Had worn them really about the same,
And both that morning equally lay
In leaves no step had trodden black.
Oh, I kept the first for another day!
Yet knowing how way leads on to way,
I doubted if I should ever come back.
I shall be telling this with a sigh
Somewhere ages and ages hence:
Two roads diverged in a wood, and I—
I took the one less traveled by,
And that has made all the difference—
Robert Frost [Chapter Eight]

RUT Rules

- RUT Rule Number One: *Innovation and leadership are grown, nurtured, and trench-tested in the routine march of mankind.* [Chapter One]

- RUT Rule Number Two*: The value of RUT travel must be recognized by the traveler before the journey can become productive.* [Chapter One]

- RUT Rule number Three: *Every RUT has an origin and a destination.* [Chapter Two]

- RUT Rule Number Four: A RUT *defined is a step in the right direction.* [Chapter Two]

- RUT Rule Number Five: *RUTs are a part of life, get over it!* [Chapter Two]

- RUT Rule Number Six: *RUTs are not to be considered diseases or dysfunctions, but simply as central to the way we "get on" with life.* [Chapter Two]

- RUT Rule Number Seven: *The only way to remedy a negative cultural (or individual) image is to redefine it, causing a re-imaging of popular thinking.* [Chapter Three]

- RUT Rule Number Eight: *I get a whole lot more accomplished—a whole lot faster—following, rather than fighting, my RUT.* [Chapter Three]

- RUT Rule Number Nine: *RUTs need management because they are much less intentional than they appear.* [Chapter Three]

- RUT Rule Number Ten: *Rest Stops are not Pit Stops.* [Chapter Three]

- RUT Rule Number Eleven: *The existence of a RUT proves motion, which is a good thing—PITs imply immobility and stagnation, which are very bad things.* [Chapter Three]

- RUT Rule Number Twelve*: A RUT Trek takes its direction from the direction someone else established ahead of you.* [Chapter Three]

- RUT Rule Number Thirteen: *RUTs by definition are designed for more than one person to Trek.* [Chapter Four]

- RUT Rule Number Fourteen: *A bunch of us can be at different locations in the same RUT at the same time.* [Chapter Four]

- RUT Rule Number Fifteen: *Teams are not about teams; they are about others.* *[Chapter Four]*
- RUT Rule Number Sixteen: *The original creator of a pathway had their own purpose or destination in mind. The important question is: Where is the RUT taking me?* *[Chapter Four]*
- RUT Rule Number Seventeen: *Good or bad RUTs are so defined by their travelers, not by their direction.* *[Chapter Four]*
- RUT Rule Number Eighteen: *Without Trail Blazing there is no RUTting.* *[Chapter Four]*
- RUT Rule Number Nineteen: *To break out of a RUT, you have to be in a RUT.* *[Chapter Four]*
- RUT Rule Number Twenty: *RUTs are forged by others to be followed.* *[Chapter Four]*
- RUT Rule Number Twenty-one: *I choose my RUT, my RUT does not choose me.* *[Chapter Five]*
- RUT Rule Number Twenty-two: *To be successful, the right people at the right time all need to be properly RUTting for any given RUT Trek to be successful.* *[Chapter Five]*
- RUT Rule Number Twenty-three: *A RUT, is a RUT, is a RUT, is a...*[82] *[Chapter Five]*
- RUT Rule Number Twenty-four: *No matter "where," it's Your RUT that will get you "there."* *[Chapter Six]*
- RUT Rule Number Twenty-five: *When a choice of RUTs is presented, a choice must be made.* *[Chapter Six]*
- RUT Rule Number Twenty-six: *RUTs require management along the entire Trek.* *[Chapter Six]*
- RUT Rule Number Twenty-seven: *The better I do at setting up my RUT, the better I'll do at deciding if my RUT needs to be changed.* *[Chapter Six]*
- RUT Rule Number Twenty Eight: *We don't get to choose our RUT Revelations; our Trek chooses them for us.* *[Chapter Six]*
- RUT Rule Number Twenty-nine: *Remember Relationship.* *[Chapter Six]*

---

[82] You get the idea.

- RUT Rule Number Thirty: *When the RUT Trek slows down, do not mistake the reduction in momentum as a signal for immediate Re-RUTting! [Chapter Seven]*
- RUT Rule Number Thirty-one: *Swapping RUTs alters the destination, not the RUT Rules. [Chapter Seven]*
- RUT Rule Number Thirty-two: *The point of breaking out of a RUT is only to forge a new RUT. [Chapter Seven]*
- RUT Rule Number Thirty-three: *Don't be easily enticed away from life's discipline only for the sake of change. The flowers and the thorns encountered in the landscape of our RUT Paths, should be considered precious gifts to guide us all to the completion of our journeys. [Chapter Seven]*
- RUT Rule Number Thirty-four: *RUTs being followed faithfully are already completed in the mindset of the Trekker. [Chapter Eight]*
- RUT Rule Number Thirty-five: *If a decision to Re-RUT is properly made, there should be no regret or guilt associated with the leaving of the former RUT. [Chapter Eight]*
- RUT Rule number Thirty-six: *The end of one RUT is the beginning of another. [Chapter Eight]*
- RUT Rule Number Thirty-seven: *The more successful I am at completing my RUT, the more confident, efficient, and productive I'll be in preparing for and completing my next RUT. [Chapter Eight]*
- RUT Rule Number Thirty-eight: Don't assume a RUT is predictable and unchanging. *[Chapter Eight]*
- RUT Rule Number Thirty-nine: *The first Trek step forward only assures an opportunity for the next Trek step. [Chapter Eight]*
- RUT Rule Number Forty: *RUTs Rule! [Chapter Eight]*

RUT Wisdom

It's not because of outside or intervening circumstances...
...It's not due to a lack of available resources...
...It's not for a lack of planning or initial commitment that
I'm distracted, or completely derailed from my track;
It's because...of ME! [Chapter Three]

My purpose has power. [Chapter Three]

The real discovery is not the creation of my uniquely individual
RUT, but in the RUT I choose to follow that starts me on
the path toward becoming a unique individual. [Chapter
Three]

It's in the "internal (mental) image" of the RUT that I either
choose to celebrate or curse my existence. [Chapter Three]

If your parents don't have children, neither will you. [Chapter
Four]

Someone was here before me; otherwise there would be no
RUT to follow. [Chapter Four]

Even though the path and direction are set, the landscape of a
RUT changes because of the travelers who touch it. [Chapter
Four]

The "team" is a bunch of individuals secretly wanting to
achieve their own secret objective using the resources of the team
which is geared toward a common objective that typically does
not have a thing to do with the individual's desired secret
objective. [Chapter Four]

FOLLOWING IS OK. [Chapter Four]

You really can lead by following. [Chapter Four]

Every Trail Blazer has also been a RUT Trekker. [Chapter Four]

Every Trail Blazer was first a RUT Trekker. [Chapter Four]

Just because I can recognize my RUT and even decide about complying with, or rebelling against its course for my destiny, doesn't mean I'll manage my Trek well. [Chapter Five]

Before jumping into the RUT with both feet, step back and make sure that it's the right RUT, with the right Trekker's with the right directions. [Chapter Five]

PITs are the camp of the undecided. [Chapter Six]

If my RUT is going to get me where I want to go, even if it's not as sexy or maneuverable as I thought it would be, then I'd spend a lot less time and arrive a whole lot more quickly if I simply stayed the course rather than investing in the quest of another route. [Chapter Six]

Indecision Pauses Purpose. [Chapter Six]

Doubt isn't the evil twin sister to faith, but its parent. [Chapter Six]

RUT Realization can be incredibly uplifting or dismally disappointing, but its result is the greatest reward ANY RUT can offer. [Chapter Six]

The dare with Revelation is having the patience to run it out—in a RUT. [Chapter Six]

If I can't get beyond the belief that mine is the ONLY Revelation, I will become a Trail Blazer—I'll have to because no one else will tolerate my company. [Chapter Six]

Other people Trekking the same RUT with me can have different revelations. [Chapter Six]

The ability to recognize where you are in your individual RUT process and then manage your individual Trek rather than trying to change everyone else's RUT to match yours: THAT's the dividing difference between RUT rapid transit and bumper cars! [Chapter Six]

The quality of your RUT Management will have little if any impact on the amount of crap that comes your way. It does however directly affect the outcome of how you deal with the crap. [Chapter Seven]

Delays, Detours, and BackRUTs are not always things to overcome quickly; they allow the Trek to be purposely slowed down. [Chapter Seven]

If you're not having conversations with yourself about the difficulty of holding true to your Trek, your RUT is worthless. [Chapter Seven]

RUTs can be dirty places. [Chapter Seven]

Moses never stepped foot in the Promised Land, but he didn't need to! [Chapter Eight]

RUTs Get Results! [Chapter Eight]

If a RUT is still a RUT by any other name, then nothing has really changed other than what you now do with the "nothing" that has really changed. [Chapter Eight]

RUT Management is the ability to plan, implement, and Trek through the course of one's own RUT journey. [Chapter Eight]

Where the Trail Blazer is important, the RUT Completer is crucial, because without the Completer's example of perseverance, none of the rest of us would truly believe the Trek could be finished. [Chapter Eight]

RUTting is all about "ALL." [Chapter Eight]

Enjoy the RUTs of your life! [Chapter Eight]

RUT Revealing Points

RUT Revealing Point Number One: *If I can't get beyond the belief that mine is the ONLY Revelation, I will become a Trail Blazer—I'll have to because no one else will tolerate my company.*

RUT Revealing Point Number Two: *Other people Trekking the same RUT with me can have different revelations.*

RUT Revealing Point Number Three: *Some people are NOT experiencing, nor have they EVER before experienced, nor might they in the future experience any Revelational RUT moments.*

RUT Lexicon

Anti-RUTists—A dangerous sect bent on the destruction of the RUT as a lifestyle. Their primary offensive tool is the demonizing of RUTs, claiming that devotion to the discipline of a completing one's Trek is an "Old-fashioned" and "Antiquated" notion.

Arrival—Completion of a specific RUT Trek. This is the ultimate and highest achievement for any RUT Trekker.

Back-RUTting—Turning back and retracing the RUT route.

Cross Purpose—The distraction caused by focusing interest on two separate RUTs at the same time.

PIT (Periodic Interruption of Trajectory) Stop—Becoming fixed in a specific location, undecided about the best direction to continue: A dangerous activity because of the potential of the Stop becoming a **Permanent Interruption of Trajectory**.

Realization—The knowledge of why the Trek is important and where the Trekker is heading which allows the Trekker to consider the original objective.

Relevance—Becoming less anxious and more excited in the confines of the RUT, allowing the Trekker to look forward to a well managed and meaningful outcome.

Reliance—Considering the RUT as a confidence building and skill-learning guide.

Re-RUTting—Veering off one RUT onto another established RUT route.

REST Stop—Stopping temporarily to rest and get bearings.

Revelation—Readily embracing the idea that the Trekker is preparing in the immediate moment for what can't possibly see *trending* beyond the horizon.

RUT (Repetitive Unchanging Trajectory)—A track or groove made by repetitive passage which can be a physical, procedural, or a metaphorical trail, mistakenly associated with boredom and monotony. RUTs are intentional with a variety of emotions resulting from their following based on the individuals management of the journey.

RUT Bumping—The attempt, when in a RUT, to randomly escape the Trek for no intentional purpose.

RUT Dissonance—The argument that goes on in your head that suggests you might have made a mistake in your choice concerning some aspect of your RUT. It is also fondly known as "blowing your brains out from the inside."

RUT Frustration Factor—Compels each person to change just for the sake of "Uncomfortableness."

RUT Imaging—The ability of mentally looking forward and backward to honestly define the track of your journey and effect its outcome.

RUT Leadership—The act of encouraging others by example to follow a specific RUT Route.

RUT Management—The identification of a RUT's qualities and the directional choices then make based on that information.

RUT Misnomers—*Trapping, Tracking, Trailing, and Trending.* The misconceived psychological images that are commonly associated with RUTs.

RUTology—The study of the RUT in motion

RUTonomics—The economy associated with RUT Trekking. The closer an individual comes to fully completing a RUT, the higher the value of that RUT to the individual and to others Trekking the same path. Re-RUTting and Trail Blazing activity by an individual negatively impact the value of the RUT that the individual is abandoning.

RUT Senses—There are seven: Sense of Comfort, Sense of Community, Sense of Confidence, Sense of Familiarity and Security, Sense of Learning and Internalization, Sense of Productivity, and Sense of Spiritual Well Being.

RUT Slow-Down—A phenomenon that occurs naturally due to delays, detours, and BackRUTs along the Trek path.

RUT's-End—Come on! Do I have to explain *this* one to you?

RUT Servitude—Cooperatively helping others achieve their goals and destinations while simultaneously reaching out for one's own brass ring.

RUT Synergy—I have to be willing to let others in my RUT pass by me in both directions, realizing that there may be another, more capable of leading than I am, who may be **RUTing** up from behind. I may have to let a former leader, who is no longer able to lead, **Back-RUT**. I can't be willing to do this so that I can move faster through the RUT, but so that the RUT works more effectively for all involved. RUT Synergy results in RUT Unity. It's really what teams were meant to be, only better…RUTtier!

RUTting—Staying in the RUT. Antonym: Trail Blazing.

RUT Unity—Allowing RUT Synergy to work for the benefit of the entire RUT population.

Team—A bunch of individuals secretly wanting to achieve their own secret objective

using the resources of the team which is geared toward a common objective that typically.

does not have a thing to do with the individual's desired secret objective.

Trail Blazing—Veering off an established RUT into completely unexplored territory.

Trek—The journey associated with using a RUT to arrive at a specific destination.

Trekking—The actual process of using a RUT to arrive at a specific destination.

Trenching In—Making the difficult decisions associated with staying in a challenging RUT.

Trench-Tested—A Solid RUT Trek that has undergone the rigors of evaluation and solid management proving to be the best path possible for the Trekker.

Printed in the United States
70413LV00002BA/226-264